ISBN 978-0-265-08605-6
PIBN 11047191

English
Français
Deutsche
Italiano
Español
Português

www.forgottenbooks.com

Mythology Photography **Fiction**
Fishing Christianity **Art** Cooking
Essays Buddhism Freemasonry
Medicine **Biology** Music **Ancient**
Egypt Evolution Carpentry Physics
Dance Geology **Mathematics** Fitness
Shakespeare **Folklore** Yoga Marketing
Confidence Immortality Biographies
Poetry **Psychology** Witchcraft
Electronics Chemistry History **Law**
Accounting **Philosophy** Anthropology
Alchemy Drama Quantum Mechanics
Atheism Sexual Health **Ancient History**
Entrepreneurship Languages Sport
Paleontology Needlework Islam
Metaphysics Investment Archaeology
Parenting Statistics Criminology
Motivational

 RANDOM HOUSE, NEW YORK

FIRST PRINTING

Photograph facing page 14 by Fred Fehl
Photograph facing page 60 by Talbot
LIFE photograph facing page 84 by Allan Grant
Photograph on binding by Talbot

MANUFACTURED IN THE UNITED STATES OF AMERICA

Pour

JOSE FERRER

Notre Quatrième Volant!
Les Spewacks

My 3 Angels was produced by Saint-Subber, Rita Allen and Archie Thomson at the Morosco Theatre, New York City, on March 11, 1953, with the following cast:

(In Order of Appearance)

FELIX DUCOTEL	*Will Kuluva*
EMILIE DUCOTEL	*Carmen Mathews*
MARIE LOUISE DUCOTEL	*Joan Chandler*
MME. PAROLE	*Nan McFarland*
JOSEPH	*Walter Slezak*
JULES	*Jerome Cowan*
ALFRED	*Darren McGavin*
HENRI TROCHARD	*Henry Daniell*
PAUL	*Robert Carroll*
LIEUTENANT	*Eric Fleming*

ADOLPHE

Directed by Jose Ferrer
Setting designed by Boris Aronson
Costumes by Lucinda Ballard

SCENE

The action of the play takes place in the family Ducotel's living room back of a general store in Cayenne, French Guiana, December, 1910.

ACT ONE

Christmas Eve

ACT TWO

Later that night

ACT THREE

Christmas morning

The single set is a living room back of a general store in Cayenne, in French Guiana. The climate is hot and humid. The room reflects the tropics, but the furniture has obviously been imported from France and bespeaks another world. An arch in the center of the back wall, hung with bamboo curtains, opens into a corridor that leads into the shop. A bell rings when someone enters the shop and this can be heard in the living room. A double door in the upstage left wall leads to the family kitchen, and a door downstage of this leads to other rooms in the house.

Facing the audience upstage, left and right of the center arch, are two doors reached by three steps leading to two guest rooms, which figure prominently in the action. A bamboo gate, stage right, leads to the garden. A ladder is featured, to the right of the center arch. It reaches to an opening in the roof. The rest of the ceiling is beamed and thatched.

In the center of the room is an oval dining table with three chairs, right, left and above the table. At right and left are armchairs. A bureau that is used for china, linen, books, papers and general catch-all is left of the center arch. Opposite the bureau hangs a hat rack and mirror. To the left of the garden gate is a commode stacked with unopened boxes and baskets. A similar stack of crates and baskets is heaped against the bamboo wall, right of the kitchen doors. An oil-lamp fixture hangs between the doors in the left wall, and on the side of the two bedroom doors hang two more such fixtures. A stand lamp is downstage of the garden gate.

There are the usual pictures and decorations on the walls. A thermometer-barometer hangs on a pole, stage right. Across the center arch is draped a piece of warm-colored material in contrast to the bamboo and raffia walls of the room.

* * * *

ACT ONE

ACT ONE

Time: Christmas Eve, 1910.

At Rise:

FELIX DUCOTEL *is sitting at the table, center, working at his ledgers, desultorily. He is in his late fifties, and is dressed for Paris rather than Cayenne. He wears a frock coat, boiled shirt, etc.*

FELIX DUCOTEL *is a thoroughly amiable and impractical soul. We hear the bell of the shop door, but* FELIX *does not. After a pause, the bell is heard again.*

EMILIE, *his wife, enters from the kitchen after second bell, carrying a bowl of fresh green peas. She is patient with her husband, for she loves him.*

EMILIE
(Seeing that he has not responded to the bell, crosses to entrance to shop)
I was sure I heard the bell, dear.

FELIX
No.

EMILIE
I was sure someone had come into the shop.

FELIX
Not a soul. Well, one hears bells at Christmas. I don't mean literally. There are bells in the air, so to speak. Sleigh

bells, jingle bells. One remembers one's childhood. Father Christmas. The angels. The three wise men. (*Mops his brow*) Very hot for Christmas, of course. (*Looks at thermometer*) One hundred and five!

EMILIE

Must you wear that frock coat?

FELIX

My dear, I have a position to maintain—as a Frenchman, as a business man, as manager of a substantial establishment in . . .

EMILIE

In a colony of convicts! (FELIX *returns to table*) Felix!

FELIX

What?

EMILIE

You don't think that bell means another sneak thief's been here?

FELIX

Why are you so suspicious? (*He pinches her cheek*) Always suspicious!

EMILIE

You ask me that here—in this colony of thieves! Desperate criminals wandering around free as air! (*Hammering is heard*) Three of them up there repairing our roof right now!

FELIX

My dear, they're perfectly honest.

EMILIE

Honest?

FELIX

They're not thieves! They're murderers.

(*Harmonica playing is heard in the garden.*)

EMILIE
(*Stunned*)

They are? Those three—on *our* roof?

FELIX

Most of them are, you know. At least so I've been told. They're excellent roofers, and considering the heat and humidity, extremely industrious.

EMILIE

Felix, did that boy ever pay you for the harmonica?

FELIX

What harmonica?

EMILIE

Felix!

FELIX

No. He's a very gifted boy.

(*Harmonica playing is louder.*)

EMILIE

He's out there now. Go out and tell him he either pays or you take the harmonica.

FELIX

(*Firmly*)

Emilie, please! (*Placing the bowl of peas on the right end of table*) I'll handle this affair.

EMILIE

How?

FELIX

It's a matter of bookkeeping.

EMILIE

Bookkeeping?

FELIX

I'll put it down to overhead.

EMILIE

What?

FELIX

In any business enterprise, one must take account of local conditions. Here in Cayenne, we have musically frustrated natives. They're starved for music, for food, for life itself. They have no money. What can one do? One puts it down to overhead.

(Hammering is heard.)

EMILIE
(Indicating roof)
Overhead! Those murderers are driving me mad—overhead!

FELIX

Overhead is a technical commercial expression.

(Hammering stops. He sighs. Bell rings.)

EMILIE

There's someone in the shop.

FELIX

Is there?

(Rises and moves toward shop. MME. PAROLE *enters. She carries an umbrella and a string shopping bag filled with parcels.)*

MME. PAROLE

Merry Christmas!

*(*EMILIE *rises.)*

FELIX

Merry Christmas, Mme. Parole.

MME. PAROLE

I only stopped by for a bottle of Chartreuse—for Ernest, you know.

FELIX
(Begins searching through boxes)

I'll get it.

MME. PAROLE
(Places bag and umbrella on table)

It's my yearly Christmas surprise for poor Ernest. He always gives me a box of biscuits. He eats them, of course, and I drink the Chartreuse.

(Hammering begins.)

FELIX
(Searching)

Let me see . . .

MME. PAROLE
(Looking up)

You still have your workmen. I must say I find convicts convenient. So cheap, and so willing. I wouldn't have any other servants. No natives for me. Take my Louis. A treasure —a perfect treasure. Immaculate, and what a cook! He may be a little peculiar—shall we say effeminate. But my dear, it takes all kinds to make a world. He doesn't bother me. And he adores Ernest.

FELIX

I don't understand it. I had a case of Chartreuse here—right here . . .

MME. PAROLE
(Taking bundle from shopping bag)
Ernest gave me your mail. Two ships came in this morning.

EMILIE

Thank you. While we're waiting—Felix was just going over the accounts—weren't you, Felix?

(Indicates books.)

FELIX
(Still searching, finds cognac bottle)
Was I? Ah, yes.

EMILIE
(Stifling her irritation)
And he thought if you could possibly . . . It's quite a large bill . . .

MME. PAROLE
But, of course. You know how scatterbrained I am.

EMILIE

That's why I took the liberty of reminding you . . .

FELIX
(Going to MME. PAROLE*)*
I'm terribly sorry, but we seem to be out of Chartreuse. I have some cognac.

9

MME. PAROLE

Cognac will do. (*Takes the bottle, puts it in shopping bag*) How much do I owe you? (*Searching in the bag*) Where's my purse? Oh! What a scatterbrain I am. I forgot! (*Getting up, preparing to leave*) Oh, well, it doesn't matter . . . charge it.

EMILIE

Well, how soon do you think you'll . . .

MME. PAROLE

By the way, how's the shop going? Better? Ernest says that you're too trusting, too careless. People take advantage. People are such beasts! Well, I must take a look at my bill one of these days. Good-bye.

(*She exits into the shop.*)

FELIX

What a scatterbrain!

EMILIE

As scatterbrained as a fox!

FELIX

(*Returning to his chair*)
I must get back to my books.

EMILIE

Books! Credit right and left, nobody pays, and sneak thieves take the rest. It's Cherbourg all over again. Thank goodness, we still have a little capital left. How much is left,

Felix? (FELIX *looks up*) Of the money we brought from home?

FELIX
Oh, that capital. That's invested.

EMILIE
Invested?

FELIX
I forgot to tell you. There was a prospector through here with a very attractive proposition. A gold mine somewhere in the west. You wouldn't understand these affairs. Believe me, I'm being practical.

EMILIE
Then all I hope is that Marie Louise marries someone completely impractical.

FELIX
Marie Louise will marry for love, just as we did.

EMILIE
God help her!

FELIX
Do you regret it very much?

EMILIE
No.

FELIX
There you are. (*Rises, moves left, mopping his brow*) We have had our ups and downs, but it's not too bad here. The

heat is a little trying, but as a practical business man I think of all the money I save in coal bills. The heat is free.

(MARIE LOUISE *enters from shop, carrying her hat, gloves and purse. She is tremendously excited.*)

MARIE LOUISE

Mama, Paul's here. (*Going to armchair to leave hat, gloves, purse.* EMILIE *turns to her*) He is on the *Mirabelle*. I knew he'd come for me. I knew it! I didn't dare breathe it, not even to you. But I knew he wouldn't wait a whole year. I knew it! Now do you believe me? Now do you think it is wrong to trust? Blindly, completely?

EMILIE

When you've simmered down, will you please tell me . . . Paul's here? Alone?

MARIE LOUISE
(*Picks up purse*)

No, with his uncle. They're in quarantine. Papa, you've got to get them right out.

EMILIE
(*Still bewildered*)

You've seen them?

MARIE LOUISE

How could I? I told you they're in quarantine. Uncle Henri sent word through M. Parole for you to get him right off the ship. Here's his note. (*Gives* FELIX *the note taken from purse*) M. Parole gave it to me. I'll give Paul my room,

12

and I suppose we'll have to give his uncle yours. I'm going to do Paul's room myself. I know just how he likes it. He's not fussy, just particular.

EMILIE

Felix . . . Did Henri write you he was coming?

FELIX

Well, not exactly . . .

EMILIE

Paul hasn't written *you*, has he, Marie Louise? It seems to me he hasn't written in months.

MARIE LOUISE

He wanted to surprise me. Paul always said letters are so banal. (*Picks up hat and gloves*) I'm going to get some flowers from the garden. Paul loves flowers.

EMILIE

Fresh sheets would be more to the point.

MARIE LOUISE

Yes. The embroidered ones. I won't tell Paul I embroidered them myself. He'll just *know*. Isn't it miraculous? Flowers in the garden for Christmas! Merry Christmas, Papa! Merry Christmas, Mama! Merry Christmas!

(MARIE LOUISE *exits to garden.*)

EMILIE

My two children . . . One I gave birth to—one I married.

FELIX

This is a terrible shock . . . You don't know.

EMILIE

What don't I know? After all, Henri has many interests in many places. This shop's a bagatelle to him. He hasn't come down here to . . . Or has he? Felix, what don't I know?

FELIX

(*Disjointedly*)

In some of his letters he threatened—unless I reorganized drastically—But how could I? With local conditions . . . He can afford to lose a little money the first year. Give a man a chance to get acclimated.

EMILIE

Felix . . .

FELIX

You'd think a man who swindled me out of a first-class department store—legally, I admit—a *cousin*—by marriage, I'll admit—but still a cousin—We grew up together as boys. . . . (*Reads the note*) "I have two days to give you. I want to make a complete inventory and check your books. I shall then make the logical decision. Be good enough to get me off this damn ship at once."

EMILIE

Logical decision? Felix, is he going to close the shop?

FELIX

I don't know.

14

EMILIE

Or get someone else?

FELIX

I don't know.

EMILIE

(*Going to him, quietly*)
Are your books in very bad shape, Felix?

(*She indicates the books on the table.*)

FELIX

Temporarily—only—temporarily—I really haven't
checked . . .

EMILIE

(*After a pause*)
We can always go home.

FELIX

With what? And to what? At my age? God help us!
(*Loud hammering*) What's that? (*Remembers the convicts*)
Oh!

EMILIE

That's not God coming to the rescue. Just some of His
wayward children who'll solve all our problems by murder-
ing us in our beds tonight. (*Embracing him*) Oh, Felix, you
should have been a poet.

FELIX

What am I going to do?

EMILIE

Do? Your going to do as he says. Go down and see the Health people and get him off the ship.

FELIX

I guess so . . .

(MARIE LOUISE *enters from garden with flowers.*)

MARIE LOUISE

Papa, haven't you gone yet? Papa, they're waiting.

FELIX

I'm going. Thank God, come what may, I still have you, Emilie.

EMILIE

You still have me, Felix. (FELIX *exits into shop.* EMILIE *goes to table and looks through bundle of letters*) Marie Louise, there's a letter here for you from Suzanne.

MARIE LOUISE
(*Takes letter*)

It's always the same silly letter. In school she was always first with the bad news. Guess who's down with the mumps. (EMILIE *picks up bowl of peas and letters, starts toward kitchen*) Guess who's going to be expelled. Guess who's pregnant.

EMILIE

Marie Louise!

(*Exits to kitchen.*)

16

MARIE LOUISE
(*Suddenly*)

I wonder if she's written me about Paul.

(*Opens letter and starts to read it.*)

(*As* MARIE LOUISE *sits down to read, three figures descend the ladder and stop. They wear pajamalike uniforms, with the appropriate numbers, straw hats and sandals.* JOSEPH's *number is 3011.* JULES' *number is 6817.* ALFRED's *number is 4707.* JOSEPH, *like* JULES, *is in his forties. He's an ex-forger and ex-promoter.* JULES *killed a faithless wife, is fairly well educated, introspective.* ALFRED, *in his twenties, is an ex-playboy who murdered for money. They watch her as she reads. She smiles. They smile. She chuckles. They chuckle silently. She rises, startled. They react. Then, suddenly, a gasp escapes her. She keels over. The three convicts move to her.* JOSEPH *puts on his glasses and picks up the letter.* ALFRED *is carrying a small cage made of a coconut shell and twigs; it has a leather handle. As he moves toward the girl, he leaves the cage on the table.*)

JOSEPH

I wonder if this letter was poisoned.

JULES

Poisoned?

JOSEPH

I read somewhere poisoned letters were common in the days of the Borgias. The victim picked it up . . . Pouf!

17

JULES

Well, nothing's happened to you—yet.

JOSEPH

No.

JULES

Damn funny . . . There she was, reading away, smiling, chuckling and then—out like a light.

JOSEPH
(*Having glanced quickly through the letter*)
Ah! Here's the poison.

(*Reads.*)

"Darling, Paul and I are engaged." Three exclamation points. Engaged, in capital letters. "Papa and M. Trochard arranged it just before Paul sailed with his darling uncle. Darling Marie Louise, I know how happy you'll be for us." Happy capitalized, two exclamation points. "After all, darling, a schoolgirl crush is not love, as we all know. And let's be frank. That's all there was between you and Paul, and honestly I don't mind. Not a bit." Two exclamation points.

(ALFRED *goes to left of* JOSEPH, *staring at the girl*)
"But I do want to save Paul embarrassment when he sees you. You know how kind"—capitalized—"how very kind he is." Want to hear any more?

JULES

No.

(*Drinking in all the details of the room.*)

JOSEPH
(*Examining envelope*)
Suzanne Audibert . . . (ALFRED *kneels to get a closer look at the girl*) Incidentally, she writes the day of her engagement her complexion cleared up completely. Putting two and two together . . . (*Feeling letter*) I should say—judging from the quality of the stationery—(*Sniffs it*) the general tone of the letter—I should say Suzanne Audibert is quite rich.

ALFRED
She's a bitch.

JOSEPH
Of course.

ALFRED
That Paul must be mad! To turn this down. (*Staring at* MARIE LOUISE) She's beautiful!

JOSEPH
Enough of that! In your position one doesn't admire a beautiful woman. Neither party stands to benefit.

ALFRED
I can look, can't I?

JOSEPH
Get me some water instead.
(*Indicates kitchen.*)

19

ALFRED

Right.

(EMILIE *enters as* ALFRED *moves to kitchen. She backs away, frightened.*)

EMILIE

Oh!

(ALFRED *exits to kitchen.*)

JULES

Don't be afraid, Madame . . .

EMILIE
(*Seeing* MARIE LOUISE)

Marie Louise!

(*Goes to her.*)

JULES

We were on that ladder when it happened.

EMILIE

Marie Louise, speak to me. When what happened?

JULES

She fainted.

JOSEPH

Nerves.

JULES

Shock.

JOSEPH

No wonder ... Read this letter ... (*Gives her the letter*) Here's the viperish paragraph. (ALFRED *returns with glass of water*) Believe me, Madame, we sympathize with you. (*Sprinkles water on* MARIE LOUISE) Uncle Henri's unexpected and unwelcome arrival. The fickle Paul! (EMILIE *returns letter to* JOSEPH. *He hands glass to* ALFRED) And she had such high hopes!

EMILIE

(*Staring at him*)

Did you hear *everything* up there?

(*Indicates roof.*)

JOSEPH

Everything.

EMILIE

Oh! (MARIE LOUISE *moans*. JOSEPH *and* ALFRED *move to ladder*) Poor darling.

JULES

She's coming around. When she opens her eyes, it *might* be a good idea if she sees you first. (*He moves up to join other two*) While we know a great deal about her, she doesn't know very much about us, and might be a little— shy.

EMILIE

Darling.

21

MARIE LOUISE
(*Sitting up*)
Where am . . . What happ . . . (*She sees men*) Oh!

EMILIE
Don't be afraid.

MARIE LOUISE
(*Getting up slowly*)
I'm not afraid. Nothing can frighten me now.

EMILIE
Marie Louise, my poor darling . . . I know what it means
to you . . .

MARIE LOUISE
Please leave me alone. I don't want to talk about it. I
don't want to talk to anybody. I don't want to see anybody.
I just want to die. (*She runs into her room*) I just want to
die.

EMILIE
Marie Louise!

(*Starts to follow her.*)

JULES
(*Stopping her*)
I'd leave her alone. Youth always dallies with suicide. We
who live on know better. Alfred . . .

(ALFRED *follows* MARIE LOUISE *into her room.*)

EMILIE

But . . .

JOSEPH

No danger. Everything's under control. Alfred's looking after her. He's quick as a cat.

EMILIE

She's so upset—so shocked . . . God knows what she might do . . .

JOSEPH

Alfred's problem!

(ALFRED *re-enters.*)

ALFRED

She's in her room. Nothing to worry about. I checked. No poison. No weapons. (*Goes to table, puts down scissors and file*) I removed these. Scissors . . . nail file . . . no sedatives . . . no gas stove, of course . . . And if she jumps, her window is only three feet from the ground.

JOSEPH
(*Extending his hand*)

Well done.

ALFRED
(*Shaking hands*)
A pleasure . . . a real pleasure . . .

(*Goes to door of* MARIE LOUISE's *room.*)

JULES

We disapprove of death. Especially for young and charming girls. She'll be all right. Time heals all wounds. We're authorities on the subject of time.

(*Shop bell rings.*)

EMILIE

Good Heavens. A customer. At a time like this. I suppose I'd better see . . .

(*Starts toward shop.*)

JOSEPH
(*Stopping her*)

A customer is always welcome. May I? It'll be a treat for me.

(*Exits into shop, leaving hat on bureau.*)

EMILIE

He's not going to . . .

JULES

Wait on the customer? Of course. There's nothing he likes better. He can sell anything to anyone—and has.

(EMILIE *looks with uncertainty from the shop entrance to* ALFRED, *then to* JULES. *There is an awkward pause.*)

JULES

We make you nervous, Madame?

EMILIE

No . . . It's just that . . .

24

JULES

You've never had convicts working for you before?

EMILIE

Never.

JULES

Our loss, Madame . . . Our loss . . .

(*Places chair beside table for her.* ALFRED *disappears quietly into* MARIE LOUISE's *room, unnoticed by* EMILIE.)

EMILIE

You don't talk like a convict, somehow.

JULES

Well, I wasn't *born* in a cell. And on the other hand, I wasn't sent here for biting my nails.

EMILIE

Somehow you haven't the face of a . . . a . . .

JULES

A murderer? I agree. That's exactly what I said when I caught a glimpse of myself in the mirror after I'd . . .

EMILIE

(*Fascinated, despite herself*)

After you'd . . .

JULES

After I'd strangled my wife, Madame.

EMILIE

Oh!

JULES

She didn't think so, either, poor thing. If she'd thought I had the face of a fool, she would have been right. I was a fool, of course. When I realized it, it was too late. There she was stretched out on the carpet, her poor thin little neck all purple, her eyes staring—in astonishment, I'm sure.

EMILIE

My God!

JULES

Exactly what I said, Madame. I called out to Him, but He was busy elsewhere.

EMILIE

Was she—a bad woman? Did she make life miserable for you?

JULES

Never! Never in six years of happy marriage. It was my fault.

EMILIE

Oh!

JULES

I came home from a trip, one day—unexpectedly.

EMILIE

Unexpectedly?

JULES

She didn't expect me . . . *He* didn't expect me . . . As a matter of fact, I didn't even expect myself.

EMILIE

Well, you did have provocation, at least.

JULES

Crime of passion . . .

EMILIE

Well . . . yes . . .

JULES

I know. That's what the newspapers called it. My attorney was eloquent on the subject. But it was stupidity, Madame. Black stupidity. I should have sent her a telegram.

(ALFRED *enters.*)

ALFRED

The patient is weeping.

EMILIE

I must go to her.

JULES

Why not let her weep?

(JOSEPH *enters from shop before* EMILIE *can move.*)

JOSEPH

Madame, can you change this, please? Take out twenty-five francs.

27

EMILIE

What did you sell?

(Goes to bureau, takes a small cash box from drawer, brings it to table.)

JOSEPH

The painting . . . Madonna with Child . . . Artist unknown.

EMILIE

The painting? It's been here as long as we have. Who bought it?

JOSEPH

The postmaster.

EMILIE

He couldn't have. He's an atheist.

JOSEPH

He wanted a bedspread.

EMILIE

And you sold him the Madonna and Child? Why, that's a miracle.

JOSEPH

No, madame. I appealed to his cupidity. I asked one simple question. How do you know this isn't a Rembrandt? Besides, I couldn't find a bedspread.

(He takes the money and exits into shop.)

28

EMILIE

(*To* JULES)

Are there very many like you in the . . .

JULES

In the Bastille? Oh, Madame, there are all kinds—a world like any other. All kinds.

EMILIE

Are you all so—busy? Selling paintings and looking after girls who've fainted?

JULES

No. Pleasant things like that don't often come our way.

(JOSEPH *returns.*)

JOSEPH

Ten francs extra, Madame.

(*Gives it to her.*)

EMILIE

Extra?

JOSEPH

For the frame . . . A painting, after all, consists of two items—the canvas and the frame. The canvas is an intangible. A matter of taste. Worth a fortune or zero. But the frame . . . Ah! That's real value. An investment.

EMILIE

I'm a little dizzy.

(*Puts money in cash box, returns it to bureau drawer.*)

29

JOSEPH
(*Spying the books on the table*)
Books! I have a passion for books. Account books. Jules, did I ever tell you about the night I had to doctor the books of a company that presumably owned three factories?

JULES
Tell Madame.

JOSEPH
They were air factories, Madame.

EMILIE
Air?

JOSEPH
Not compressed air. Just air. For invalids, convalescents. It was a marvelous idea.

EMILIE
I'm afraid I don't understand.

JOSEPH
Quite simple. As you know, doctors prescribe a change of air for their patients. Well, lots of people can't afford the Riviera or Switzerland. So we had factories at these resorts, where the air was bottled. Just as you bottle mineral water.

EMILIE
Oh!

JOSEPH
We had two kinds of bottles—big ones to change the air of an entire room and the handy pocket-size inhalators!

EMILIE

And people bought these bottles?

JOSEPH

We never put the product on the market. But we had a large group of stockholders.

JULES

A very large group, Madame. Until the judge ordered a change of air for *him*—and here he is!

JOSEPH

The judge, unfortunately, was one of our stockholders. Well, shall we run along?

(*Goes to ladder.*)

JULES

I guess so ... (*To* ALFRED, *who seems far away*) Alfred! (ALFRED *starts*) Come on.

(ALFRED *picks up the coconut cage from table and passes* EMILIE.)

EMILIE

What have you got in there? (*He shows it to her*) Oh, a snake! What a horrible creature!

ALFRED

Why, that's Adolphe. He's our pal.

EMILIE

Is he poisonous?

JOSEPH
(*Moving to* ALFRED)

Deadly.

JULES

We're very fond of Adolphe. Last year when we worked in the jungle, we used to be watched by a guard . . .

JOSEPH

Extremely unpleasant man and, unfortunately, incorruptible. Spurned all bribes. A combination of honesty and brutality, Madame, is unbearable.

JULES

He loved to treat us like slaves—while he lolled under the trees, in the shade. Well, one morning this little fellow dropped down from a branch right on to his red neck. (*Snaps fingers*) Adolphe's a pal . . . Well, let's get going.

ALFRED
(*Suddenly, as they turn toward ladder*)

Wait a minute . . .

(*He quickly hands* JULES *the cage and goes into* MARIE LOUISE'S *room.*)

EMILIE

Where's he going?

JULES
(*As he turns to her, he places the cage on the bureau*)

Perhaps you'd better go, too, Madame. I think your daughter may need you now. (EMILIE *hurries into* MARIE LOUISE's *room*) Alfred must have heard something. Did you?

JOSEPH

No.

JULES

I didn't hear a thing.

JOSEPH

Ah, youth! Keen ears—keen eyes. Of course, Alfred's the athletic type. (*With a glance toward the books on the table*) My exercises were always mental.

(EMILIE *returns.*)

EMILIE

I don't understand it. She's not in her room—her window's open . . .

JULES

And Alfred?

EMILIE

I didn't see him.

JOSEPH
(*Going to gate*)
Her window opens on to the garden.

EMILIE

Garden?

JULES
(*Suddenly*)
The river! Right off the garden.

(EMILIE *moves to go.*)

EMILIE
I must stop her.

JOSEPH
She's been stopped.

EMILIE
By your friend?

JULES
Of course.

JOSEPH
(*Reporting from the lookout*)
She's arguing.

EMILIE
I'm going to her.

JOSEPH
Too late.

EMILIE
Too late?

JOSEPH
Alfred won the argument. (*He laughs*) He's convinced her.

EMILIE
Are you sure?

JOSEPH
(*Laughing as he goes to the table*)
Alfred has a striking eloquence. Your daughter, Madame,
is no longer thinking of ending it all. In fact, your daughter
is no longer thinking.

EMILIE
What?

JOSEPH
Knockout!

(*Sits in chair at table, examining the books and
papers.*)

EMILIE
What?

(*Starts toward gate.* JULES *stops her.*)

JULES
Only thing to do, Madame. If she jumped in the river,
what would Alfred do? Jump, too. And then—she would
struggle. He'd use the approved technique of knocking her
out before he could swim back with her. The technique's
just as effective ashore, and dryer.

(ALFRED *enters from the garden, carrying a limp*
MARIE LOUISE.)

ALFRED
All present and accounted for.

(*His hair is mussed, his face scratched.*)

35

EMILIE

Marie Louise!

ALFRED

She's all right, I assure you, Madame, as a sportsman.
Pulse normal. I pulled my punch, of course.

JULES

Your efficiency is monotonous.

JOSEPH
(*Straightening up books, papers on table*)
I really don't approve of all this disorder.

EMILIE
(*To* ALFRED)

Oh! You're bleeding.

ALFRED

A scratch or two.

EMILIE

How could Marie Louise . . .

ALFRED

She wasn't herself, Madame.

EMILIE

Let me put some iodine on it. In this climate the slightest
cut becomes infected.

> (*Exits to kitchen.* FELIX *enters from shop, hangs up
> his hat, moves down in time to see* ALFRED *carrying*
> MARIE LOUISE *toward her room.* JULES *blocks his
> way.*)

FELIX

Marie Louise! What are you doing with my daughter? Come back here! (*Goes toward shop, calling*) Police! Police! (ALFRED *carries* MARIE LOUISE *into her room*) Kill me, but spare them . . . That's all I ask. Police! Police!

EMILIE

(*Re-entering*)

No! No! Felix, not the police!

(FELIX *crosses back to* JULES, *trying to get around him.*)

FELIX

Marie Louise, your father's coming to defend you . . . Courage . . . Courage . . .

(ALFRED *re-enters.*)

EMILIE

You don't understand, Felix.

FELIX

What don't I understand?

EMILIE

He *had* to hit her.

FELIX

Hit whom?

EMILIE

Marie Louise.

37

FELIX

Why?

EMILIE

She scratched him.

(*Goes to* ALFRED *to treat the scratch.*)

FELIX

Are you mad? (*Going to her*) Defending this—this—
beast! Nursing him like a Florence Nightingale! (*Turns to
see* JOSEPH *very busy with the papers, goes to him*) What
are you doing with my papers?

JOSEPH

If you'll forgive me for saying so, I find unspeakable con-
fusion. There's a place for everything and everything has its
place!

FELIX

What? What the devil do you . . .

EMILIE

(*Goes to him, takes his arm*)

Please, Felix.

FELIX

But . . .

EMILIE

(*To convicts as she pulls* FELIX *toward* MARIE LOU-
ISE's *room*)

Don't go before my husband comes back. He'll want to
thank you.

38

FELIX

Thank them?

EMILIE
(*Pushing him ahead of her*)
You don't know what we've been through. Just come along. I wonder if a hot compress . . .

(FELIX *exits.*)

JOSEPH

Cold, Madame. As cold as the climate will permit.

EMILIE

Thank you.
(*She exits.*)

ALFRED
(*Dreamily*)
You know . . .

JULES

What?

ALFRED

That girl's light as a feather.

JULES

Forget her! Remember! We have one advantage — and only one—over other people. We can live without emotion. We can achieve serenity.

JOSEPH

You'd better achieve some serenity pretty damn quick.

JULES
(*Sitting*)

It seems to me I've been searching for serenity all my life. I never really wanted love. I wanted domesticity. Serenity again, you see.

JOSEPH

I have no passions—none—except . . . (*Shop door bell rings*) A customer! (*Rises, but hesitates*) Should I?

(*His eyes glow.*)

JULES

Oh, go on, enjoy yourself.

JOSEPH

Just this once. ·

JULES

Why not?

(JOSEPH *exits to shop.*)

ALFRED
(*Moving toward shop*)
He really gets a kick out of it.

JULES
(*Looking around*)
It's wonderful, isn't it?

ALFRED

What?

JULES

A home!

ALFRED

Oh, yes.

JULES

Flowers ...

ALFRED

Yes ...

JULES

That chair . . . a picture . . . the evening paper. Her knitting ...

(EMILIE *enters, followed by* FELIX.)

EMILIE

My husband has something to say to you.

(*After a warning glance back at* FELIX, *she exits into room.* JULES *rises.*)

FELIX

My wife's just told me . . . I apologize for the misunderstanding . . . for my outburst ... where's that other fellow?

(JOSEPH *returns from the shop, carrying a white linen jacket over his arm.*)

JOSEPH

The customer wants a larger size—14. This is a 12.

FELIX

I don't believe I have a 14.

JOSEPH

You don't. That's why I told him I'd get one back here—from stock.

FELIX

From stock? I have no clothing stock back here.

JOSEPH

I know that. I don't sell a piece of goods. I sell an idea. I'll just take this one right back to him.

(*He exits into shop.*)

FELIX

But . . . He's out of his mind. The man'll know it won't fit. He can see—feel it . . .

JULES

He won't see or feel anything. He won't get a chance to.

FELIX

But it's not fair—it's not ethical . . . Of course, I suppose you fellows aren't concerned with ethics, naturally. I mean— I don't want to hurt your feelings.

JULES

Not at all. No, some of us are downright crooked. Our world's just like yours. All kinds. The only difference is we were caught.

FELIX

Oh, yes. My wife told me, and I wanted to thank you. I'd like to repay you.

JULES
Not necessary.

ALFRED
Wouldn't dream of it. It was a labor of love.

(JULES *looks at him.*)

FELIX
Well, my wife thought . . . I'm not sure it's a practical idea . . . In fact, I'm not sure it's not . . .

ALFRED
What'd she have in mind?

FELIX
I know it's impossible. But she thought if you wanted to—and could spend the evening here—since it's Christmas Eve and all that . . .

JULES
(*Touched*)
That's very kind of her—very kind . . .

(JOSEPH *enters, shows* FELIX *the money.*)

JOSEPH
Sold! Fits him like a glove when he doesn't button it. (*Goes to bureau, puts money in cash box*) Oh, yes, I sold him some cleaning fluid for the spots.

FELIX
There were spots? The coat was spotted?

JOSEPH

I made the spots myself. A little grease. The spots explain the bargain.

FELIX

Bargain?

JOSEPH

At the regular price of 27 francs, he wouldn't touch that jacket; but at the reduced price of 27 francs, he snapped it up.

JULES

Joseph, the gentleman has invited us to spend Christmas Eve here.

FELIX

Well, my wife thought . . .

JOSEPH

An enchanting prospect!

FELIX

Of course, I realize you can't . . .

JULES

Oh, but we can. We accept.

ALFRED

With thanks.

FELIX

But won't the authorities object? They'll miss you at roll call!

ALFRED

They'll forgive us!

JOSEPH

It can be arranged.

FELIX

It can? I must warn you—I haven't any spare beds . . .

JOSEPH

We're insomniacs.

JULES

Do you know what an armchair means to us?

JOSEPH
(*Quickly appraising the chair*)

Imitation Louis Sixteenth.

FELIX

And I must warn you. My wife hasn't prepared anything special. You know how expensive fowl is.

JOSEPH
(*With a knowing look to* JULES *and* ALFRED)

Christmas dinner without a turkey or at least a chicken? (*Shop doorbell rings*) Another customer! Business is brisk tonight.

(*Starts toward shop.*)

FELIX
(*Preceding him*)

If you don't mind . . .

45

JOSEPH
What?

FELIX
Allow me!

JOSEPH
By all means. (FELIX *glares at him and exits into shop. A look of disappointment comes over* JOSEPH.) I'll just coach from the sidelines. (*Exits into shop.* JULES *returns to his chair.*)

ALFRED
Who gets the chicken?

JULES
(*Goes toward garden*)
I'll get it.

ALFRED
I'll set the table. Pick a plump one.

JULES
One takes what one finds.

(*He exits to the garden.* ALFRED *begins setting the table. He takes the ledgers and papers to the bureau. Then he removes the brocaded cloth from the table, folds it, and places in on a tall basket standing near the bureau.* MARIE LOUISE *enters from her room, carrying a small suitcase, hat, gloves, etc. She's obviously leaving. She stops as she sees him.*)

MARIE LOUISE

Still here?

(*She puts down hat and bag, and puts on gloves.*)

ALFRED

How many for dinner tonight? Let's see. There's your father, mother, Uncle Henri, Paul, you . . .

(*Gets dinner cloth from bureau, opens it onto table.*)

MARIE LOUISE

I'm not having dinner. I'm leaving tonight.

ALFRED

You are?

MARIE LOUISE

Oh, don't worry, I won't try it again. I'm going to the Dominican convent first. Then, I'll see. (ALFRED *gets plates from bureau, sets them*) The Mother Superior'll understand. My life is finished. (*Picks up bag and hat, starts toward shop*) At least, I can be of service to others.

ALFRED

(*Arranging plates*)

You want to sit next to Paul, of course . . .

MARIE LOUISE

(*Stops*)

I told you I won't be here. How dare you meddle in my affairs?

ALFRED

I asked a civil question. I don't get it. A man travels on a stinking ship for weeks to see you—and you run away from him. (*He gets silver from bureau drawer, sets places*) You're mad about this man. You don't want to live if you don't get him. He's here. He wants to see you . . .

MARIE LOUISE

See *me?*

ALFRED

Why did he come if he doesn't want to see you? You believe that Suzanne? A fellow doesn't travel four thousand miles just to prove he's a liar.

MARIE LOUISE

His uncle made him come.

ALFRED

Where's your trust? Your faith? How do you know there's a word of truth in what she says? And if there is—and a marriage has been arranged—how do you know he isn't coming here to explain, to make plans to *disarrange* it — get around his uncle, with your help, your support, your *love* . . .

MARIE LOUISE

Oh, no.

(*Puts down hat.*)

ALFRED

It's not impossible, is it?

MARIE LOUISE
(*Turns to him*)

Do you honestly think so?

ALFRED

Would he come all this way just to get his face slapped?

MARIE LOUISE

I wouldn't slap his face. He knows that. I don't go around slapping faces.

ALFRED

Oh, I don't know.

(*Feels his scratch and gets cups and saucers from bureau, sets them.*)

MARIE LOUISE

I'm sorry—I'm terribly sorry—about that.

ALFRED

Forget it.

MARIE LOUISE

You really think . . . Of course, there may be something in what you say. He's come to explain—to . . .

ALFRED

Now shall I set a place for you?

MARIE LOUISE

Funny! I believe you because I *want* to believe you. And yet I *know* . . .

ALFRED

Give the fellow a chance! I'll tell you what. Heads you go, tails you stay. (*Picks up plate*) Let's toss a plate.

MARIE LOUISE

No, no, I'll stay.

(*Puts down bag.*)

ALFRED

Your mother almost lost a plate.

(JOSEPH *enters from shop carrying a peignoir on a hanger and a nightcap. He goes to table, and to himself, counts to ten on his fingers. Then he hurries back into the shop to complete the sale. After his exit,* ALFRED *gets glasses from bureau, sets them.*)

MARIE LOUISE

Tell me . . .

ALFRED

Yes?

MARIE LOUISE

I know I shouldn't ask . . .

ALFRED

They all want to know. Why was I shipped here?

MARIE LOUISE

Was it a political crime?

ALFRED

Politics? Women? Yes. Horses? Yes. Politics? No! (*Gets the cruet from bureau, sets it in center of table*) I never was interested in politics. Anyway, I've never held with the anarchists. What's the point of shooting one scoundrel? Another will come along to take his place.

MARIE LOUISE

Were you . . .

ALFRED

Framed? No, I was guilty as hell.

(*Gets napkins from bureau, sets them.*)

MARIE LOUISE

You stole from somebody?

ALFRED

Yes.

MARIE LOUISE

You were hungry!

ALFRED

I'd just finished a magnificent dinner in Maxim's with a woman who . . . Well, I thought at the time she was the most beautiful woman I'd ever seen. We were *friends*. To keep her friendship — you'll pardon me — to keep *her* — I needed my stepfather's generosity. As long as my mother was alive, he was generous enough. I went to see him.

MARIE LOUISE

Yes . . .

ALFRED

I really went to see his safe. I knew he had negotiable securities, jewels, money . . .

MARIE LOUISE

Oh!

ALFRED

Unfortunately, he was a light sleeper. He suddenly appeared in the library. He was a very imposing figure, my stepfather. Legion of Honor. Very deep voice. Old soldier. He roused the servants, called for the police. I lost my head. I killed him.

MARIE LOUISE
(*Gasps*)

How could you?

ALFRED

With a poker, Mademoiselle.

(*She is horrified. He goes to chair, picks up her hat and suitcase. JULES enters with a struggling chicken, which he keeps shoving under his pajama jacket. ALFRED exits to her room.*)

MARIE LOUISE
(*Startled by the noise and fluttering of the chicken*)
Oh!

(*JULES exits into kitchen as FELIX enters from the shop.*)

52

FELIX
(Going toward her)

My poor Marie Louise.

MARIE LOUISE

I'm all right now, Papa. Funny . . .

FELIX

What?

MARIE LOUISE

I can hope again.

FELIX

Of course. Of course.

MARIE LOUISE

He gave me hope.

FELIX

Who?

MARIE LOUISE

A murderer!

FELIX

Huh?

(EMILIE *enters.*)

MARIE LOUISE
(Going to her)

Oh, Mama!

EMILIE

Yes, dear?

53

MARIE LOUISE
(*Embracing her parents*)
We're going to have a lovely Christmas.

EMILIE
Of course, we are.

(ALFRED *enters, takes in the situation, goes to chair,
and carries and places it at the table.*)

MARIE LOUISE
We're going to be very festive—very gay. (*The family
group move to the table*) I shall sit next to Paul. His uncle,
of course, will sit over there . . . His uncle will grunt as he
always does . . . Paul will be so tactful, as he always is . . .
(ALFRED *carries chair and places it at the table, then picks
up footstool and places it against wall*) Then we'll drink lots
and lots of wine—especially his uncle. And he'll turn mel-
low gradually and begin to laugh. We'll sing, and then we'll
leave Paul alone with his uncle. And Paul'll say: You see,
sir? Our love is steel. No one—no one can break it.

EMILIE
Yes . . .

FELIX
The only thing is . . .

MARIE LOUISE
What?

FELIX
They won't be here for dinner.

54

EMILIE

They won't? They have other plans? So much has happened I forgot to ask you if you'd got them out of Quarantine.

FELIX

Well, as a matter of fact, I didn't see the Health people. I — I thought it over. It occurred to me . . . Well, I just couldn't face it tonight . . . And they'll be comfortable on the ship.

EMILIE

Oh! Well, we'll get their rooms ready after dinner in any case. They're sure to be here by morning.

MARIE LOUISE

And I wanted to see Paul—tonight.

FELIX

You'll see him tomorrow. (ALFRED *goes to table*) You can dream about him tonight.

MARIE LOUISE

I've dreamt so long.

(ALFRED *picks up two settings, returns them to bureau.*)

EMILIE

Well, with or without Paul, we still must have dinner, and I'd better see to it.

(*The harmonica is heard from the garden.* EMILIE *exits to kitchen as* JULES *enters. He goes below table,*

55

brushing chicken feathers from his hands, and exits into garden. ALFRED *goes to table and returns one of the chairs.)*

FELIX

(As ALFRED *takes other chair from table)*
I may be selfish, but I know I'm not sorry to be alone in the bosom of my family. *(Sees* ALFRED *as he is placing chair)* Well, practically alone. *(*ALFRED *picks up chicken feathers from floor)* That reminds me—we ought to get the tree out. Young man . . .

ALFRED

Yes, sir?

FELIX

Can you open that box?

(Indicates a box standing on commode.)

ALFRED

Got a poker? *(*MARIE LOUISE *starts)* No, a chisel would be better.

FELIX

Over there. In that drawer.

*(*ALFRED *goes to drawer, takes out chisel, begins to open box.)*

ALFRED

Right! Here we go.

(Harmonica is heard.)

56

FELIX

I suppose I should do something about that harmonica, but it's Christmas Eve.

ALFRED

(*Takes out small, untrimmed tree*)
Here's our tree. They got this one young.

MARIE LOUISE

It's beautiful.

ALFRED

And here are the trimmings.
(*Taking them from box.*)

MARIE LOUISE

It's France! It's home!

ALFRED

Uhuh.

MARIE LOUISE

That lovely pine fragrance we knew as children—in the forest near the sea . . .

ALFRED

Uhuh.

(JOSEPH *enters from garden with another tree, larger and trimmed.*)

JOSEPH

Oh, you *have* a tree!

FELIX

Where on earth did you get *that?*

JOSEPH

I'd better return it.

(*Starts to exit, stops, swaps trees, exits to garden with the small tree.* JULES *enters from garden with an orchid and a camellia. Harmonica stops suddenly.*)

EMILIE
(*From kitchen*)

Felix, Felix.

(*She enters.*)

FELIX

Yes, my dear?

EMILIE

Felix, I found a chicken in the oven. Where did it come from?

JULES

Praise the Lord, from Whom all blessings flow.

EMILIE

Oh!

JULES
(*Handing it to* FELIX)

An orchid for Madame . . .

EMILIE
(*As* FELIX *hands it to her*)

For me?

JULES

And a camellia for the young lady.

MARIE LOUISE

Why, thank you.

EMILIE

I've never seen a more beautiful orchid, except in the Governor's garden.

JULES

Neither have I.

(*Goes to tree. He,* ALFRED *and* MARIE LOUISE *add more trimmings.* JOSEPH *enters from garden.*)

JOSEPH

M. Ducotel, the young man out there has just paid for his harmonica.

FELIX

Paid?

EMILIE

How on earth did you . . .

FELIX

But, he has no money.

JOSEPH

(*Examines both*)

Of course not. We bartered. The young man wore a hand-some gold ring. You get the handsome gold ring. (*Extends it to him*) Sometimes we don't sell. We barter.

FELIX

But how do I know he didn't steal the ring? After all, receiving stolen property . . .

JOSEPH

He made that ring himself — out of a gold nugget he found. He's always finding things—nuggets, watches, bicycles. How can you doubt his word of honor? Really! To besmirch the reputation of an altar boy! On Christmas Eve!

(*He exits to garden. The harmonica is heard again.*)

EMILIE

Felix, get a bottle of wine.

FELIX

Of course.

(*He looks for wine, finds a bottle in basket.*)

ALFRED
(*Indicating tree*)
Shall we put it on the table?

MARIE LOUISE

Let's!

JULES
(*Carrying it to table*)
Here—let me—Ah! A real tree! A real Christmas in a real home!

(ALFRED *takes cruet to bureau, picks up corkscrew, gets bottle of wine from* FELIX, *opens it, then hands bottle to* JULES. *He places it on table.*)

MARIE LOUISE

Careful now . . .
(*Making room on table.*)

JULES

We place it here—tenderly.

EMILIE

I've got to go back to the kitchen.
(*Starts.* MARIE LOUISE *gets the three-angel decoration from bureau, takes it to table.*)

JULES
(*Stopping her*)

Oh, no, Madame. Tonight we are going to prepare, cook and serve your dinner. Tonight we are your servants. (*Places chair for her. She sits.* JOSEPH *enters from garden*) Beautiful! I've commissioned our young minstrel to play Christmas carols.
(ALFRED *brings wineglasses from bureau to table.*)

JOSEPH
(*Seeing the wine, picks up the bottle, examines the label*)

A Beaujolais! Not bad! May I?

MARIE LOUISE

Please.

61

JOSEPH
(*Pours a glass*)

Color perfect. Bouquet exquisite. (*Tastes the wine*) Mmm! Ah . . . '97 . . . Bottled the same year I was! (*Hands* JULES *the bottle*) I once organized a winery that was the marvel of the trade. Chateau Joseph. We had no wines, no bottles, not even a cork. But the labels were museum pieces! The Prosecuting Attorney gave me a one-man show.

(JULES *has poured for the others. Harmonica playing is quite loud now.*)

MARIE LOUISE

Listen!

ALFRED

What?

MARIE LOUISE

He's playing: Three Angels.

JULES

So he is. That was my wife's favorite Christmas carol.

(*The three convicts are standing together.*)

MARIE LOUISE
(*Singing*)

Three Angels came that night . . .

ALL
(*Joining*)

That holy night . . .

62

MARIE LOUISE

(*Picks up the three-angel decoration, goes to front
of table and places it on the top branch of tree*)
And look! Look at the tree! We have three little angels
on the tree, just as in the song. Only my angels are a little
—shopworn—a little . . .

JOSEPH

A little unlucky, Mademoiselle. They were damaged by the
long rough journey here—bruised by unfeeling hands. Fallen
angels, Mademoiselle.

MARIE LOUISE

I don't care. (*Lifting her glass, toasting the tree*) I'm going to drink to—to—my three angels.

JOSEPH—JULES—ALFRED

Thank you, Mademoiselle.

She turns to them. They toast her, and all drink as

THE CURTAIN FALLS

ACT TWO

ACT TWO

At Rise:
Several hours later.
The table has been cleared. The boxes and baskets have been taken off the commode, and the decorated Christmas tree placed there. Otherwise the room arrangement is the same as in the previous act.

JULES is sleeping in his armchair. ALFRED is stretched out on the floor near the gate, the coconut cage near him.

JOSEPH is asleep in a chair, his head on the table. The lamps are turned low and the moonlight illuminates the room and the sleeping figures.

We hear thunderous knocking on the outside door of the shop. The knocking is repeated. JULES is the first to wake. He yawns and stretches, goes to the lamp on the left wall, turns it up. The knocking is heard for the third time, louder. He goes to JOSEPH and wakes him.

JULES

Someone's trying to get in.

(Turns lamp up.)

JOSEPH

Huh? Probably the Three Wise Men paying us the traditional visit.

(Knocking is heard again, still louder.)

67

JULES

Impatient, aren't they?

JOSEPH

I'll take a look.

(*He goes into shop. Presently an angry voice is heard.*)

HENRI
(*Off stage*)

Are they deaf in there? Where the devil is everybody?

(ALFRED *wakes, gets up, joins* JULES, *puts cage on commode.*)

JULES

Doesn't sound like the Three Wise Men to me.

(JOSEPH *holds aside the bamboo curtains.* HENRI *and* PAUL *enter. They react to the two men in prison uniform.* PAUL *carries two suitcases.* HENRI *carries his portfolio.*)

HENRI

What the devil . . . Convicts!

JULES

At your service, sir.

HENRI

It was so damn dark in the shop I didn't see . . .

(*Puts hat and portfolio on table.*)

PAUL

Neither did I, Uncle Henri.

JOSEPH

(*Enters after them and joins other two convicts*)
Allow me to introduce myself. I'm 3011. (*Indicates number on his jacket*) My good friend 6817 . . .

JULES

Enchanted.

JOSEPH

And my esteemed colleague 4707.

ALFRED

How are you?

(*FELIX enters, wearing robe, as though he had dressed hurriedly.*)

FELIX

I thought I heard the bell . . . Henri!

HENRI

Good evening. Or rather good morning.

FELIX

(*Embracing them*)
My dear Henri . . . Welcome. Welcome. My dear Paul, welcome. Welcome . . . (PAUL *puts bags on floor near ladder*) I had no idea you'd come tonight. No idea, I assure you. Naturally we'd have waited up for you. (HENRI *sits*

near table. PAUL *places chair for him, then hangs their hats on pegs*) Marie Louise was very anxious to see you, Paul ... Expected you for Christmas dinner . . . Keenly disappointed.

HENRI

Was she? And were you . . .

FELIX

What, Henri?

HENRI

Keenly ‚disappointed?

FELIX

Well . . .

HENRI

Did you get my note?

FELIX

Well . . .

HENRI

Don't lie.

FELIX

Henri, I never lie. You know that. I don't know how I manage it, but I never do.

HENRI

I asked you to use your influence with the Health officials. Did you?

FELIX

Well—Christmas Eve and—all that—You know how it is —I thought—you'd be better off on the ship.

HENRI

They said you hadn't been near them. And if I hadn't threatened to have them all fired, we'd still be on that garbage scow they call a ship.

PAUL

The heat was stifling.

HENRI

(*Opens portfolio, arranges papers*)

A drunken cab driver was inflicted upon us. Even his horse was drunk! By great good fortune we managed to weave our way here without being killed. We are then greeted by your retinue of servants. (*Indicates the three*) I congratulate you upon your ménage!

FELIX

Ménage?

HENRI

Don't tell me they're not your servants. Whar are they? Your friends who are spending Christmas Eve with you?

FELIX

Well, as a matter of fact, they are—in a way.

JOSEPH

(*Coming forward*)

The boss means a good servant is always a friend. A bad servant is bound to be an enemy. He'll not only ruin your digestion. He'll even squeal to the police. Believe me, I speak from bitter experience.

HENRI

Have our bags taken to our rooms.

FELIX

Certainly. Emilie has given you these rooms here. I hope you'll forgive the primitive quality of our hospitality. Marie Louise fixed her room for you herself, Paul. I'll take your bags.

(*He's about to pick up bags when* ALFRED *forestalls him.*)

ALFRED

Allow me . . .

HENRI

(*To* PAUL)

Paul, go with him and be sure and lock your door when you retire.

PAUL

Yes, sir.

(*Exits into room, followed by* ALFRED.)

HENRI

I'm no more timid than the next man, but these fellows look dangerous. (JOSEPH *smiles at* JULES) I suppose you always go armed.

FELIX

No.

HENRI

Well, I intend to sleep with a revolver in my hand. (*To convicts*) Bear that in mind.

72

JULES

Yes, sir.

HENRI

You too!

JOSEPH

Yes, sir. We clean, oil and polish revolvers—part of our daily impeccable service.

HENRI

You won't get your hands on mine. (*To* FELIX) The rest of our luggage is in the shop.

FELIX

I'll get them.

JOSEPH

Allow me.

(*Exits to shop.*)

JULES

Would the gentlemen care for something to eat?

HENRI

You're the cook, I suppose.

JULES

Yes, sir.

FELIX

He's very good. He did a chicken with almonds tonight that was superb.

HENRI

You dined well?

FELIX

Oh, very well.

HENRI

Congratulations! I had a nauseating dinner. Chicken with almonds! Business is suddenly booming, I take it.

JULES

Chickens cost nothing here.

HENRI

Bring me some fruit.

(PAUL *enters, carrying suit.*)

JULES
(*Starts toward kitchen*)

Very good, sir. (*Turns to* PAUL) And you, sir, would you care for something to eat?

PAUL
(*Hesitating*)

I'm famished. What have you got?

(*Places suit on chair.*)

HENRI

Whatever it is, have it brought to your room.

PAUL

Sir?

HENRI

I want to have a little talk with Felix.

PAUL

Yes, sir. I wouldn't mind some cold chicken.

JULES

Yes, sir.

(*Exits to kitchen.*)

HENRI

Good night, Paul.

PAUL

Good night, sir. (ALFRED *enters*) You there . . . (*To* ALFRED, *picking up suit, tossing it to him, then exits to room*) I have a suit for you to press.

(JOSEPH *enters from shop with bag.* ALFRED *exits with bag, after swapping the suit for the bag.* JOSEPH *continues to study* HENRI *after throwing suit on chair.*)

HENRI

You!

JOSEPH

Yes, sir?

HENRI

Get out!

75

JOSEPH

How can I resist such a cordial invitation?

(*Exits to kitchen, followed by* ALFRED, *who re-enters.*)

HENRI

(*Staring after them*)

Assassins!

FELIX

They're really not bad fellows. For criminals, I mean.

HENRI

Now, let's get right down to it. I have very little time to give you. I have a factory to inspect and some mines. I have only two days here. Now . . .

FELIX

Henri, you're tired—it's awfully late—hardly the time to talk business . . .

HENRI

I'm not talking business—yet. I've sent Paul to bed so that you and I can straighten out this nonsense without a lot of silly chatter.

FELIX

Nonsense?

HENRI

I suppose you know Marie Louise had an affair with Paul before she left.

76

FELIX

Affair?

HENRI

At least I assume there was an affair. You are fortunate there were no consequences.

FELIX

Good God!

HENRI

At least I assume there were no consequences. You're not a grandfather, I take it.

FELIX

Do you mean to tell me . . . Are you implying . . .

HENRI

So there the matter rests. You may be an idiot, but even you must know I would never tolerate such a ridiculous marriage for Paul who is, at the moment, my legal heir. So if you're dreaming of a return to France via Marie Louise— wake up! I don't blame you for trying. I don't blame Marie Louise. As a matter of fact, I find the matter amusing. Where the devil's my fruit?

(MARIE LOUISE *and* EMILIE *enter. They have dressed hurriedly.*)

FELIX
(*Miserably*)

Emilie, Henri's here.

EMILIE

How are you, Henri?

HENRI
(*Rises*)

Good to see you, Emilie. You, too, Marie Louise. (*He kisses their hands*) You look charming.

(EMILIE *joins* FELIX.)

MARIE LOUISE

Is Paul . . .

HENRI
(*Sits*)

Gone to bed.

MARIE LOUISE

Oh! Did you have a good trip?

HENRI
(*Sardonically*)

Delightful.

MARIE LOUISE

Was Paul seasick? He's such a poor sailor. I remember once he took me sailing, and it wasn't really rough at all, but poor Paul suffered so, we came right back. He was furious with himself.

HENRI

You little fool.

FELIX
But just a moment . . . The child merely . . .

EMILIE
There's no need to insult my daughter, Henri.

HENRI
I have no patience with fools, male or female. Paul's engaged. Damn good family and a damn good business. I couldn't buy old Audibert out. So I'm marrying him. The girl's a cow, but she'll give milk.

(FELIX *turns away in embarrassment.* HENRI *returns to his papers.*)

MARIE LOUISE
Oh!

EMILIE
If you'll excuse us, we're going to bed. Good night, Henri.

HENRI
Good night.

EMILIE
Come, Marie Louise.

MARIE LOUISE
(*With dignity*)
Good night, M. Trochard.

HENRI
Good night, Marie Louise.

(EMILIE *and* MARIE LOUISE *go out.*)

FELIX

(As HENRI *makes no move)*

I must register my protest against your rudeness—your—your—insults—your—your arrogance! You had no right to upset Marie Louise—and her mother. Marie Louise is a very sensitive girl. A good girl.

(His voice breaks.)

HENRI

Dear, dear.

FELIX

(Drawing himself up)

It's very late. If you'll excuse me, I'm going to bed.

(Starts.)

HENRI

I'm not excusing you. (FELIX *stops*) I'm not at all sleepy. Now that I've disposed of the affair Marie Louise, let's get down to business. How's it going?

FELIX

Well, I've spent the first year getting adjusted — acclimated. Getting used to local conditions, so to speak.

HENRI

And are you acclimated?

FELIX

I think you'll find the second year a great improvement. A great improvement. I know the obstacles, so to speak. I know the market . . .

HENRI

You do?

FELIX

Oh, yes.

HENRI

How much business did we do last month?

FELIX

Last month?

HENRI

(*Impatiently*)

November!

FELIX

November?

HENRI

November's always preceded December. Let's have the figures for November, if you don't mind?

FELIX

I don't remember.

HENRI

Where are the books? Look up the figures, man.

FELIX

I'm not sure what the figures are. I haven't added up the totals yet.

81

HENRI

It's the twenty-fourth of December—technically the twenty-fifth—and you haven't closed your books for November?

JOSEPH

(*Entering from kitchen, carrying large piece of cardboard and bamboo stick*)
Of course we have, sir.

(FELIX *turns in surprise.*)

HENRI

What do you know about it?

JOSEPH

I'm the bookkeeper, sir.

HENRI

The bookkeeper! Congratulations. How much did you embezzle last month?

JOSEPH

Our gross receipts were thirty-two thousand, eight hundred and fifteen francs and forty-two centimes, sir. An advance over the preceding month of exactly eight thousand, five hundred and eighty-one francs and two centimes.

HENRI

An advance?

JOSEPH

Our figures for October were twenty-four thousand, three hundred and forty seven, and forty-eight centimes. (*Showing cardboard*) I am preparing a chart—a graph. You'll forgive the crude quality of cardboard and ink. Would you mind? (FELIX *holds one end.* JOSEPH *uses pointer*) You will observe here that business declines steadily—in the first few months — due to new management — conservative clientele skeptical of anything new, et cetera—then observe that suddenly in August — with the reawakening of confidence — M'sieu's grasp of the affair, et cetera—the line rises, steadily up, up, up, up—I expect—and I am a cautious observer—a record breaker for December . . . Right up here. I'll need more cardboard.

(*He indicates the line has run off the cardboard. He places the cardboard and pointer back of bureau.*)

HENRI

It's fantastic. A convict accountant. Charts, graphs. He knows more about the business than you do.

JOSEPH

The boss has more important things on his mind.

HENRI
(*Laughs*)

Did you hear that, Felix? You have more important things on your mind.

JOSEPH

He creates policy—guides, directs.

HENRI

Really? Tell me, Felix, it is still your policy to extend credit right and left?

FELIX

Well . . .

JOSEPH

Certainly not, sir. The boss always says that giving credit to a customer is like making him a gift of the merchandise.

HENRI

You said that, Felix.

FELIX

Well . . .

JOSEPH

The boss always says: I'm a business man, not a philanthropist. Let others play Santa Claus. I'll play safe. Hard as a rock, the boss. He has one God—cash on the line.

HENRI

Perhaps I never appreciated you, Felix. But I doubt it.

FELIX

Just a moment . . .

HENRI

What about shortages?

JOSEPH

Inconceivable. The boss has an eye like a hawk.

HENRI

Losses due to thefts?

JOSEPH

Try it some time.

HENRI

What's that?

FELIX

As a matter of fact, I've just had some trouble about a case of Chartreuse—which did disappear mysteriously and...

JOSEPH

Pardon me, sir. The Chartreuse was delivered by mistake to the Café de la Poste. I forgot to tell you. These bungling wholesalers! Call themselves merchants! No system, no organization. If you knew the difficulties the boss has to contend with!

HENRI

Well, we'll see when we take inventory tomorrow . . .

(*Closing his portfolio.*)

JOSEPH

Inventory—tomorrow? But, sir! You realize tomorrow is Christmas! A holy day!

HENRI

Good. Then the shop will be closed, and we won't be disturbed.

FELIX

Can't we wait until the day after . . .

HENRI

The day after I'm devoting to somewhat more substantial matters. I've some mines to look into. (*Rising*) We'll go over everything tomorrow. I hope, for your sake, everything's in order. Where do I sleep?

FELIX
(*Pointing to room*)
In here, Henri.

HENRI
(*Going to room*)
Good. I rise at six. We can start at seven — promptly. Good night.

(*He exits into room.*)

FELIX
(*To* JOSEPH)
Have you gone mad?

JOSEPH
Sir?

FELIX

Fake charts — graphs — preposterous statements. I didn't have sense enough to stop you. Or the courage.

JOSEPH

The situation seemed to call for boldness—and a little exaggeration.

FELIX

It's not enough to pull figures out of the air — concoct stories about the Café de la Poste. I must produce books to-morrow—and the stock . . .

JOSEPH
(*Smiling*)

Oh, books!

(*Goes to bureau, gets ledgers.*)

FELIX

What do you mean: "Oh, books!"

JOSEPH
(*Bringing the ledgers to the table*)
We have all night to straighten those out.

FELIX

It'll take more than one night.

JOSEPH

You don't know my system of inspired accounting. (*Goes to bureau for inkwell and pens*) Trouble with most business-men is they think mathematics is a science. With me, it's an art.

FELIX
(*As it dawns on him*)

You mean . . .

JOSEPH

Sir, doctoring your books will be a delightful treat for me!

FELIX

I wouldn't dream of falsifying—any statements.

JOSEPH

Let me explain: Sir, in business, as in life itself, we have reality, and we have the *appearance* of reality. Now you're a painfully honest man. But your books make you look like a crook. All I want to do is to make your books reflect *you* —the real you. I want to paint your portrait.

FELIX

That's all very well, but . . .

JOSEPH

For example, you might have drunk the Chartreuse yourself or given your missing Swiss watches to some little native girl.

FELIX

I happen to be a devoted husband and father.

JOSEPH

Not in your books. In them you're a waster, a lecher, a scoundrel. I want to restore your character. And in presenting a picture of a prosperous establishment, I want to restore your confidence, your faith in yourself, your morale as a manager. Armed with my books, you'll go forth and make the books come true! And now—with your co-operation . . .

(*He prepares to go to work.* HENRI *enters in his dressing gown.*)

HENRI

I thought I'd find you still up.

FELIX

(*Startled, going to him*)

Can I get you anything, Henri?

HENRI

Just your books.

FELIX

My books?

HENRI

The accounts.

FELIX

Oh, yes—the accounts.

HENRI

Don't tell me you want to do a little work on them. I'll keep them in my room tonight. I want them just as they are now—in all their pristine purity.

FELIX

Henri, your suspicions are . . . are . . .

(*He stops.*)

JOSEPH

(*Assembling the books*)

I'm sure the gentleman will apologize in the morning, but if it's the books he wants, sir, the books he shall have.

HENRI

Are they all there?

JOSEPH

Yes, sir. I'll put them in your room. (*At the door*) The fourth page is loose.

(*Exits.*)

HENRI

You don't seem to share your accountant's confidence?

FELIX

Well . . .

HENRI

Let's hope I can say I'm sorry in the morning.

(*As* HENRI *reaches the door to exit,* JOSEPH *opens door. He fills the narrow doorway so that* HENRI *cannot pass.* JOSEPH *turns sideways, but this does not create any more space. Realizing the impasse,* JOSEPH *backs in the room to allow* HENRI *to exit. Then* JOSEPH *enters, closing door behind him.*)

JOSEPH
(*Admiringly*)

Sharp as a razor, isn't he? I thought of dumping the books in water—making the ink run, the figures blur—but he'd have caught on. He's so damn suspicious. Besides, there was no water in there.

FELIX

I'm relieved.

JOSEPH

Relieved?

FELIX

Yes. Because I was tempted. I might have let you doctor the books. I would have lived to regret it.

JOSEPH

Regret?

FELIX

Oh, I know I'm ridiculous. But I still have honor left.

JOSEPH

There must be something that could be done.

FELIX

I forbid you to do anything.

JOSEPH
(*Impressively*)

Do you realize, tomorrow morning, at seven, a tornado will roar out of that room . . .

FELIX

I know.

JOSEPH

And you're not afraid!

FELIX

Of course, I'm afraid. If I were put upon a wild stallion, the fear of falling off would not make me a horseman. You see, I don't know how to ride. I'm an honest man. I don't say that boastfully. Nor apologetically. I state a fact. I don't know how to be anything else.

JOSEPH

Isn't that interesting? My dear sir, you're a phenomenon!

FELIX

You may laugh at me, but that's the way I am. I'm going to bed. I think I may even sleep. In fact, I'm sure I will. For an honest man I am a dreadful liar. How can I close my eyes tonight? What's to become of us? And Marie Louise —Paul didn't even ask for her. Good night!

(*Exits. In the pause that follows,* JOSEPH *devises a plan. After a look in the direction of the room that houses* HENRI, *then toward* PAUL's *room, he quickly puts on his glasses, goes to the bureau for writing paper, returns to the table and begins writing.* JULES, *carrying a plate with a chicken wing, followed by* ALFRED, *enters from kitchen, headed toward* PAUL's *room.* JOSEPH *interrupts them. They stop.*)

JOSEPH

What have you got there?

JULES

I'm bringing the young man his cold chicken.

(*Holds up chicken wing.*)

JOSEPH

Pretty small portion.

JULES

All that's left. Alfred ate the leg just now. He wasn't hungry—just malicious.

(*A big grin from* ALFRED.)

JOSEPH

We can't offend the young man with such measly hospitality. Besides, he shouldn't be thinking of food at a time like this.

(JULES *puts plate on table.*)

ALFRED

That's what I say! Here he is under the same roof with a girl who adores him, worships him . .

JOSEPH

The situation is in hand.

JULES

What's up?

JOSEPH

We arrange a meeting. At once.

JULES

Huh?

JOSEPH

Too bad I haven't got a sample of the young man's handwriting.

JULES

Handwriting?

JOSEPH

So I'm printing it.

(*Reads the note he has written*)

"My darling! My own! Come to me! I wait! I tremble! Oh, my adorable, my beloved! I shall always be your Paul." Alfred, give this to her. Her room is back of her parents' room. Be quiet as a cat.

ALFRED

Right.

(*Takes note and exits.*)

JULES

She's not sleeping. I'll guarantee that.

JOSEPH

You get the young man.

(JULES *goes to door and knocks.* JOSEPH *returns paper to bureau.* PAUL *emerges in robe.*)

PAUL

Yes?

JULES

Pardon me, sir. I'm awfully sorry, but there's no cold chicken left.

PAUL

Oh, what a nuisance!

94

JOSEPH

It wouldn't have been cold in any case. You know what
our climate is like. We blow on all our food to cool it.

PAUL

Well, damn it, haven't you got anything else?

JOSEPH

We have warm centipede.

PAUL

What?

JULES

A native delicacy.

PAUL

I'd rather go to sleep hungry.

(*Starts to room.* JULES *stops him.*)

JULES

Sleep? You haven't seen *her* yet.

PAUL

What?

JOSEPH
(*Walking with him*)

Do you think *she's* sleeping?

PAUL
(*Staring from one to the other*)

Marie Louise?

95

JOSEPH

Who else?

JULES

She needs you, my boy. She needs you desperately. She loves you.

PAUL

What the devil?

JOSEPH

She waits! She trembles! She pants!

JULES

Be young, young man. There's so little time.

(ALFRED *enters, followed by* MARIE LOUISE. *He moves quickly out of the way, so that the girl is standing alone near the door.*)

JOSEPH

What a coincidence! Here she is!

(JULES *and* JOSEPH *join* ALFRED.)

PAUL

Marie Louise . . .

MARIE LOUISE

Paul, dear, dear, Paul . . .

(*She runs to him, throws her arms about him. Mission accomplished, the three convicts quietly go into garden.*)

PAUL

I . . . Uh . . .

MARIE LOUISE

It's been so long . . .

PAUL

Marie Louise, my dear . . .

MARIE LOUISE

I couldn't sleep . . . I couldn't think . . .

PAUL

Neither could I, of course. It's been a wretched trip. Wretched. The God-awful heat—the filth—and Uncle Henri isn't the easiest traveling companion in the world.

MARIE LOUISE

Tell me everything.

PAUL

Everything? Well, where does one begin?

MARIE LOUISE
(*Sighing relief*)

And to think I doubted you—for even a moment. That Suzanne . . .

PAUL

Oh, Suzanne . . . Well . . . Uh . . .

MARIE LOUISE

How could I have been so blind? Why couldn't I see for myself you wouldn't have come four thousand miles just to hurt me?

PAUL

If you only knew how I had to scheme and wangle to come at all!

MARIE LOUISE
(*Going to him*)
How did you manage it?

PAUL

Persistence—patience—tact. It wasn't easy, but one manages when one loves (*Holding her*) If you only knew how I ache for you, hunger for you . . .

MARIE LOUISE
Then marry me—now—here . . .

PAUL
(*Steps away with a look toward* HENRI's *room*)
Now? Here?

MARIE LOUISE
What does it matter what he thinks? What can he do? Fire you? Disinherit you? What does that mean?

PAUL
(*Turning away*)
But my darling . . .

MARIE LOUISE
(*Moving close*)
We're young. We'll get along somehow. I don't mind cooking and scrubbing—for you.

PAUL

I know, but . . .

MARIE LOUISE

And you'd find *something* to do. There are plantations. You can be a supervisor. Ride about in a pith helmet, looking very beautiful, and ordering people about.

PAUL

I don't know anything about plantations.

MARIE LOUISE

You'd learn.

PAUL

And this frightful heat.

MARIE LOUISE
(*Going to him*)

There are the mines. They're cool. You could manage a mine.

PAUL

My dear Marie Louise, I'm thinking of you. Is it fair to condemn you to a life of—well, this sort of thing? You're entitled to a decent home, servants—Paris . . .

MARIE LOUISE

That'll come later. When you've become a huge success—at something—anything. I don't mind waiting. I don't mind waiting forever.

99

PAUL

But I do. I love you too much to condemn you to this wretched life here. No, my darling, it isn't as simple as you think. Oh, I've given it a lot of thought, believe me.

MARIE LOUISE

At home you had to fight him alone. Here you have me to help you.

PAUL

Exactly.

(*He kisses her.* HENRI's *door opens. He carries one of the account books. He sees them, stops, closes door.*)

HENRI

Charming! (*The two separate quickly.* PAUL *almost leaps*) Well, Paul, since you have so much excess energy, I suggest you expend it on something useful—these accounts. They're a mess. I want a report on them in the morning. Go to your room.

(*Gives him book.*)

MARIE LOUISE
(*Moving up to block his way*)

Paul, don't go!

PAUL

Sir, I wanted to explain . . .

HENRI

Didn't you hear me? Go to your room!

100

PAUL

Yes, sir.

(*He goes toward room.* MARIE LOUISE *is still standing where she blocked his way before. He cannot look at her. After a pause, he circles her and exits into his room.*)

HENRI

Now you listen to me, young woman. (*She stops*) Apparently I didn't make myself clear earlier. For the rest of my stay—twenty-four hours precisely—I don't want you to exchange one single word alone with Paul. Is that clear?

MARIE LOUISE
(*Turns to him*)

That's what you want—yes. That's clear. What's also clear is you've frightened Paul—made him timid, abject, servile. How could you?

HENRI

You're wasting your time. I'm not going to let Paul make an ass of himself. He owes you nothing. It takes two to indulge in these little affairs. If your parents had taken proper care of you, it wouldn't have happened. (*Stops, eyes her shrewdly, curiously*) I take it you *have* had an affair.

(*The* THREE ANGELS *appear at garden gate.*)

MARIE LOUISE

That's not true!

HENRI

You resisted—bravely? Be that as it may . . .

MARIE LOUISE

I didn't want our love to be furtive—and cheap. I wanted everything—or nothing. I still do. Paul understands. It's difficult for him because he's a man, but he understands.

HENRI

Be that as it may—(*The* THREE ANGELS *open gate and enter the room*) I suggest you turn your attentions elsewhere. You can find yourself a young man — or an older man. I suggest an older man with a little money in the bank whom you can hoodwink into an ironclad religious ceremony. On the other hand, if ceremonies don't interest you, but the comforts of life do, I should say your future was very bright. Very bright indeed. (*Now the three convicts move slowly forward.*) You're young—pretty . . . You have a desirable air of innocence . . . (*As he turns away from her toward his room, he sees the men*) What the devil do you want? (*Convicts do not move*) Are you all deaf? (*Silence. Finally, he turns to* MARIE LOUISE) Well, I've nothing more to say to you, in any case. Good night.

(*He exits into his room.*)

MARIE LOUISE
(*Quickly going to them*)

There's something I must know—now. I can't sleep until I do.

JOSEPH

Yes?

MARIE LOUISE

I must see Paul—now. Tonight!

102

JOSEPH
(*Indicating bedroom*)

Go ahead!

MARIE LOUISE

I can't go to his room. I want you to tell him I'm waiting in the garden. Please hurry.

(*She exits to garden.*)

JULES
(*To* ALFRED)

Go get him.

JOSEPH

Wait a minute! I wonder if this is wise.

JULES
(*Shrugs*)

Who knows? She wants him. She shall have him.

JOSEPH
(*To* ALFRED)

Go get him.

(ALFRED *goes into* PAUL's *room.*)

JOSEPH

I'm not sure she's going to be grateful to us for this.

JULES

Perhaps she's impatient to know the worst.

JOSEPH

The young man—and mind you, I'm pretty tolerant—is even more of a stinker than I thought.

JULES

Perhaps he's just cautious. Let's be fair. Caution is a virtue I've learned not to despise.

(ALFRED *enters with* PAUL. *He pushes him forward.* PAUL *is in his shirtsleeves.* ALFRED *carries his jacket, stands blocking the door to his room.*)

ALFRED

Come on.

PAUL

Where are you taking me?

ALFRED

Get going.

PAUL

What do you want?

JULES

We're concerned with your happiness, my boy.

PAUL

What?

JOSEPH

Someone is waiting for you in the garden.

JULES

Under the bougainvillea. Hurry.

PAUL

Marie Louise?

JULES

Correct.

PAUL

(*Looking from one to the other*)
I warn you! (*Looks about*) I'm going to call for help.

JOSEPH

Just because you're asked to meet a lovely girl in the garden on a gorgeous tropical night? Gentlemen, what has happened to France?

PAUL

I have work to do—the accounts . . .

JULES

Accounts? Can this be our youth?

PAUL

This is sheer insanity. (*Starts to room, but can't get by* ALFRED. *He turns back*) What the devil are you interfering in my life for? This is grotesque!

JULES

You forget it's Christmas.

PAUL

What?

105

JOSEPH

You're our Christmas gift to the young lady.

PAUL

You're mad! What can I say to her?

JULES
(*Going to him*)

Whatever she wants to hear—that you love her.

JOSEPH

You *do* love her?

PAUL

Of course I love her. I've told her that.

JOSEPH

Tell it to her again.

JULES

Women never get bored with repetition of the simple trite phrase: I love you. They supply their own variations on the theme.

JOSEPH

Exactly. Let her do most of the talking. Occasionally you may be called upon to say: "Yes, my love!" And occasionally you will say: "Always and forever." Since it's dark, she won't be able to see your face and know you're lying.

PAUL

I'm not my own master. She doesn't understand that I *can't* marry her.

JOSEPH

Let's live for this night only. Let's leave the future—to the future. I suggest you kiss her . . .

ALFRED

What for?

JULES

It's customary!

JOSEPH

Kiss her frequently—and tenderly.

JULES
(*Moving close to him*)

Behave out there as if this were the most important, the most beautiful, the most cherished moment of your life.

PAUL

But Uncle Henri . . . Is he asleep? Awake? What if . . .

JOSEPH

We'll take care of Uncle Henri. Go! Think of *her* for once. We want to give the young lady an hour's happiness— and it seems to me we're giving you a pleasant interlude. You ought to be damn grateful.

PAUL
(*Finally*)

Very well, I'll go.

JOSEPH

Bravo!

(ALFRED *steps down, holds jacket for* PAUL *to get into.*)

PAUL
(*Smiles, puts on his charm*)
And I *am* grateful—

(*Exits to garden.* JULES *goes to gate to watch* PAUL *off stage.*)

JOSEPH

We make progress.

JULES
(*Shrugs*)

It's what she wants.

ALFRED

Women!

JULES

Don't you think they ought to be chaperoned?

JOSEPH

Chaperoned?

JULES

She's overwrought — they have only this night — perhaps their last night—the garden—the moonlight . . .

ALFRED

I'll break every bone in his body.

(*Exits to garden.*)

JOSEPH

That is not the function of a chaperon!

(*Follows* ALFRED *out into the garden.* JULES *closes the gate, then slowly goes to his chair and stretches out in it. During this, church bells are heard chiming. After a pause he gets up and goes to the door of* HENRI's *room, and peeks through keyhole.* EMILIE *enters, to find* JULES *at* HENRI's *door.*)

EMILIE
(*Amazed*)

What are you doing?

JULES

Two o'clock and all's well. Our dear uncle sits with one hand clutching the bedpost as if it were a competitor's throat. With the other, he slashes at your husband's books with a pencil. He's broken three pencils in the past two minutes.

EMILIE

Where's Marie Louise? She's not in her room.

JULES

She's—around.

EMILIE

She's not in the garden with that young man, is she?

JULES

As a matter of fact, she is.

EMILIE

At this hour?!

JULES

Don't be afraid, Madame. They're being chaperoned.

EMILIE

Chaperoned?

JULES

Properly. My friends are out there.

EMILIE
(*Moving toward garden*)

Marie Louise!

JULES

Please, Madame, why spoil the happiness she's been dreaming about for so long?

EMILIE
(*Turning to him*)

She's only a child.

JULES

Only in your eyes. And if you must think of her as a child, then, Madame, remember it's Christmas. Children want toys for Christmas. Let her have her toy.

EMILIE

This is a very dangerous toy.

JULES

Why break her heart? No, it's better to let her have her

toy, until in the natural course of events it gets broken, and she'll no longer care.

EMILIE

If I only knew what to do!

JULES

Believe me, I've given the matter considerable thought in the last few minutes. You see, Madame, I'm playing father to the child I never had.

EMILIE

Oh!

JULES

(*Moving toward chair*)

I sit in this armchair, with my eyes closed, and imagine myself the head of this house.

EMILIE

Poor man.

JULES

We must see her through this trying moment, Madame. Patiently. One false step—and she's lost. Go to bed, Madame.

EMILIE

I won't sleep.

JULES

You must. You owe it to her. There's nothing you can do tonight, believe me. We're here.

EMILIE
(*Staring at him*)
As I listen to you—look at you—I don't know whether I'm awake, or asleep and dreaming.

JULES
Good night, Madame. (EMILIE *exits.* JULES *closes his eyes.* ALFRED *and* JOSEPH *enter. He opens his eyes.*) How's it going?

JOSEPH
Beautifully.

ALFRED
(*Looking off stage to garden*)
He's a cold fish.

JOSEPH
On the contrary, I'll admit that at first it didn't sound promising.

JULES
And then . . .

ALFRED
He sat there—mumbling about his damn uncle.

JULES
And then?

JOSEPH
Then they were silent. They looked at the stars.

ALFRED
Not a word from him! Like a mute! *Then* he talked.

Dribbled. He's quoting poetry right now. It took him all
this time!

JOSEPH

Some men respond slowly. Be fair, be tolerant. (JULES
goes to his chair, sits) I had the feeling that if the boy were
free to think for himself, one could hope . . .

JULES

Really?

ALFRED

He's a spineless flounder.

JOSEPH

You're prejudiced. I tell you the boy wouldn't be half
bad without his uncle. (*Indicates* HENRI's *room*) One man
capable of so much mischief.

ALFRED

Yeah.

JOSEPH

Ironical, isn't it? He's free and we're in prison. There's no
justice.

JULES

Let's bring him to justice. The case of humanity versus
Henri Trochard! Bring in the prisoner. (ALFRED *goes to
chair, places it facing upstage, in the area between the table
and the chair* JULES *is sitting in. Then he goes back to table. To* JOSEPH) Proceed, Mr. Prosecuting Attorney.

113

JOSEPH

Stand up! Do you deny the evidence? Hurry up! I haven't got all year.

JULES

Please, this is a solemn occasion.

JOSEPH

I'm in a hurry! I need another conviction. I am ambitious. I mean to be Prime Minister some day, or at least Deputy Administrator of Outdoor Comfort Stations.

ALFRED

I object.

JULES

Sustained.

JOSEPH

Overruled.

JULES

I am the Judge.

JOSEPH

I'm in a hurry.

JULES

Mr. Defense Attorney.

JOSEPH

Gentlemen of the Jury — I say to you my client is no criminal. He is a patriot. He has contributed to the greater glory of our beloved country.

JULES

How?

JOSEPH

Who cares? Gentlemen of the Jury, I say to you my client is directly responsible for the tremendous increase in our country's birth rate. Consider how he overworks and underpays his many employees. After a fourteen-hour day, do they patronize the haunts of sin, the theatres, the concert halls, the cafés? No. They totter home to their wives and enjoy the only diversion left open to them. Vive la France.

JULES

Prisoner, stand up! A stupid jury which understands nothing of the nature of man nor of the world he lives in, has found you guilty as charged.

> (HENRI's *door opens and he enters, stares at them for a moment. He carries a sheaf of papers. He goes to* PAUL's *room.*)

HENRI

Paul . . . Paul . . . (*Tries the door, opens it, goes in.* JULES *returns the chair to place at table.* ALFRED *goes to gate.* HENRI *re-enters*) Where's my nephew?

JULES

Isn't he in his room?

HENRI

He is not. And you know he's not. Where is he?

JOSEPH

If you must know, he's in the garden, with the young lady. They make a charming couple. (HENRI *moves toward garden.* ALFRED *blocks his way*) They don't wish to be disturbed. This is their moment.

HENRI

Out of my way. I've had just about enough of your damned impertinence.

(*Reaches in his pocket. Obviously doesn't find what he's looking for.*)

JOSEPH

Alfred, the gentleman is looking for something.

ALFRED
(*Producing gun*)

This, sir?

HENRI

Give me that.

(*He snatches it.* ALFRED *doesn't resist.*)

ALFRED

I cleaned it.

JOSEPH

It was in dreadful shape. The barrel was filthy. Naturally we removed the cartridges. We had to . . . They were damp anyway.

JULES

The climate, you know.

JOSEPH

Frightful.

JULES

Very unhealthy.

JOSEPH

I'd never bottle this air.

(HENRI *meanwhile examines gun and confirms the facts. He puts gun back in pocket.*)

HENRI

You've got your nerve, you scoundrels!

JULES

You've no use for a revolver anyway.

JOSEPH

We're here. We'll protect you lovingly. We make ideal watchmen! We never sleep. Twenty-four-hour service!

HENRI

I'll have you all arrested in the morning.

(*Convicts laugh.*)

JOSEPH
(*Indicates* JULES *and* ALFRED)

I'm afraid you're much too late. They've been arrested permanently. I'm only in for a brief twenty years. Sounds long, but when one thinks geologically—historically—a mere flicker of time.

HENRI

Murderers!

ALFRED

Correct!

JOSEPH

Except for me. I was like yourself—a business man.

HENRI
(*Turns to him*)

You're a thief.

JOSEPH

You're not very polite. I don't think I want to take inventory for you tomorrow!

HENRI

Don't worry. You won't.

JOSEPH

God knows I've taken inventory with all kinds of people. But one draws the line somewhere, and I draw the line at you.

HENRI

I'll settle your hash in the morning. They have ways of punishing scoundrels like you. I'll see to it that you pay for this outrage. I'll report you to the Governor—first thing in the morning.

(*Exits into his room, slamming door. In the pause that follows,* JOSEPH *goes to his chair.* JULES *goes to* HENRY's *door.*)

ALFRED

He's going to see the Governor in the morning.

JULES

Sixty days solitary . . .

JOSEPH

Or six months in that hellish jungle. (*Shudders*) I'm not normally a pessimist, but I say again: There's no justice.

ALFRED

No.

JULES

Sixty days solitary, if we're lucky.

JOSEPH

If only our dear uncle would disappear! Vanish!

JULES

Yeah.

ALFRED

He's human.

JOSEPH

I doubt it.

ALFRED

I still say he's human. Know what I mean?

JULES

Know what he means?

JOSEPH

Now, gentlemen, please, I'm not a man of violence. Anything physical is repugnant to me. Besides we may get caught.

ALFRED

Well?

JOSEPH

I want to live.

ALFRED

Why?

JOSEPH

I want to know what tomorrow will bring.

ALFRED

I know now.

JOSEPH

There are other tomorrows. Listen to me! I have a plan. If you help me escape . . .

JULES

Yes?

JOSEPH

I'll go to Cherbourg . . .

ALFRED

Well?

JOSEPH

I'll assume another name, another personality.

JULES

And then?

JOSEPH

I'll go to work for him and at the end of a year he'll go bankrupt and blow his brains out.

JULES

It doesn't sound very practical to me, your plan.

ALFRED

Always the promoter—escape—bankruptcy—a year. I'm a man of action.

JULES

Just a moment . . .

ALFRED

You're not weaseling out, too?

JULES

No.

ALFRED

Well, let's go.

JULES

Just a moment. Every man's entitled to a fair trial.

JOSEPH

He's already had his.

JULES

True.

(*They think.*)

JOSEPH

How? That is the question.

ALFRED

Simple.

JOSEPH

How?

ALFRED

Adolphe!

JOSEPH

Adolphe!

JULES

Of course.

JOSEPH

An inspiration! Quick, humanitarian and safe.

ALFRED

An accident.

JULES

Only too common in the tropics.

ALFRED

Here we go!

(*Rises, picks up coconut cage from commode, goes below table to door of* HENRI's *room.*)

JOSEPH

An accident is about to be arranged.

JULES

Let justice be done.

ALFRED

Go, Adolphe! (*Opens the box against a crack in the door*) Right through the crack. Go, Adolphe!

JOSEPH

Has he gone?

ALFRED

(*Looks into cage*)

Gone.

JULES

(*With glee*)

I bet he's climbing right up the bed. Right up the post. Adolphe sees the hairy hand. The hand opens palm up, as if to say: I want mine. All right, says Adolphe. You can have it all. Keep the change.

JOSEPH

Funny, I never thought of it.

JULES

What?

JOSEPH

A snake farm. There's a fortune in it! Think of the demand. Think of all the relatives in the world who want to get rid of other relatives.

JULES

Hear anything?

ALFRED

Not a sound. Trust Adolphe. He's a quiet worker.

JULES

As the presiding judge, I should note the exact time of execution.

JOSEPH

Let's not be bureaucratic. Shall I say a few flattering words about the deceased?

JULES

No.

JOSEPH

It's customary. (*Rises*) I was thinking of something like: He was a devoted bachelor and an uncle.

(ALFRED, *who has been peering through the keyhole, turns back.*)

124

MY 3 ANGELS

ALFRED

I can't tell if he's asleep or dead.

JOSEPH

I have an infallible test. Rattle a few coins.

ALFRED
(*After another look*)

Hasn't moved.

JOSEPH

We shall know in the morning.

(*During the following speech, ALFRED goes to the lamp on the wall and turns it down. Then, to the other lamps, turning them down. He then stretches out on the floor, prepared to sleep.*)

JULES
(*Quietly as he gets up*)

Those who should be asleep are asleep. Those who should be dead are dead. (*Looking off stage*) Our young lovers are neither dead nor asleep. Just half way between, as they should be.

(*He stretches out in his chair. As ALFRED turns down the last lamp, JOSEPH, who has been sitting quietly, thinking, gets up and moves to bureau, where he picks up a stack of writing paper, inkwell and pens, and brings these supplies to the table.*)

JULES

What are you going to do?

125

JOSEPH

I'm going to write the last will and testament of Henri Trochard.

He puts on his glasses, sits and prepares for his new task as

THE CURTAIN FALLS

ACT THREE

ACT THREE

At Rise:

The next morning.

Early morning sun is pouring into the room. ALFRED *is still asleep.* JOSEPH *is seated at table with collection of pens, inks, paper, and laboriously writing.* JULES *enters from kitchen with coffee, cheese and bread on a tray.*

JULES
(*Placing tray on table*)
How's it coming?

JOSEPH
The last will and testament of the deceased is practically ready. One more sentence and I'm finished.

JULES
One more sentence and we're all finished.

JOSEPH
Please! It's too early in the morning for your morbid fancies!

JULES
(*Pouring coffee for the three*)
Anyway, you're enjoying the job.

129

JOSEPH

(*Showing letter*)

Why not? This is my masterpiece! Here is the note from dear Uncle Henri. Here's *my* sample effort. Compare! Ink, handwriting! Perfection!

JULES

Don't ask me. I'm no expert.

(*Takes his and* ALFRED'S *mugs, goes to* ALFRED, *wakes him.* ALFRED *sits up, drinks.*)

JOSEPH

I challenge the experts! There isn't a court in France that won't honor the deathbed request of our poor old uncle.

(*Reads.*)

"My conscience has been bothering me grievously of late. I have a curious premonition of death, somehow. I am writing this shortly after midnight and ask that this constitute a codicil to my will. If anything should happen to me, I implore my nephew, Paul, to restore to Felix Ducotel, my cousin, the Gallery Moderne in Cherbourg, which I acquired by sharp practice. I could not face the judgment of Providence if this were not done. Paul, you are my heir, and I beg you to help a repentant and tortured sinner by making generous amends to my cousin, Felix.

(*So moved by the following sentiments that a tear comes into his voice.*)

Please, Paul, respect my wishes. Be happy, Paul, as I was not. Be honest, Paul, as I was not. . . .Henri Trochard."

JULES

Be happy! Be honest! Damn good advice to a young man

starting out in life with a fortune. And easy to follow for a young man with a fortune.

JOSEPH

I'm deeply moved by the old sinner's sudden repentance. It just goes to prove . . .

JULES

What?

JOSEPH

There's a little good in the worst of us. After all, he had a conscience!

JULES

You gave him one. A beauty!

JOSEPH
(*Modestly*)
It was nothing, really. Nothing at all.

(*Dunks his bread in coffee, proceeds then with his work.* ALFRED, *having finished his coffee, places mug on table, then goes to chair and picks up the coat of* PAUL'S *suit that has been there since the previous act.*)

JULES

By the way . . .

(*Dunking his bread in coffee.*)

JOSEPH

Yes?

JULES

Before you finish his will . . .

JOSEPH

Only a codicil—technically.

JULES

Don't you think it would be a good idea to make sure the deceased—is dead?

JOSEPH

I have the utmost confidence in Adolphe. I'm sure everything went according to plan. Incidentally, we must get Adolphe back to his cozy little nest.

JULES

As soon as I finish my coffee, we'll take a look.

(ALFRED *takes off his convict's coat and slips into* PAUL's *jacket.*)

ALFRED

How do you like me?

JOSEPH

Splendid!

ALFRED

(*Going to mirror*)

He's got a good tailor. I once had a wonderful tailor. I think I still owe him some money.

JOSEPH
(*Working*)
Naturally! You were a gentleman!

ALFRED
(*Stroking cloth*)
Feels good. Look at that lining. (*Strokes lining*) Feels like a woman's skin.

JULES
Why torture yourself?

ALFRED
No harm in pretending I'm human again.

JULES
You're an adolescent.

ALFRED
That's what my stepfather used to say! "Grow up!" he used to say. You know, I was thinking out there—it' all *his* fault.

JULES
Whose?

ALFRED
My stepfather's.

JULES
Because you smacked him over the head with a poker?

133

ALFRED

I wouldn't be just wearing Paul's jacket. I'd be in Paul's shoes. If it weren't for the old bastard.

JULES

I don't follow you.

ALFRED

Look! That night I dined with Jeannine at Maxim's. Suppose the old bastard were a different kind of old bastard. A real *father*. Someone like you. (*Indicates* JULES) I'd come up and see you. I'd say, "Good evening, sir."

JULES
(*Entering into spirit of the thing*)
What do you want now, you young scoundrel? More money?

ALFRED

How'd you guess, sir?

JULES

A girl, I suppose.

ALFRED

Yes, sir.

JULES

Sowing a few wild oats, eh?

ALFRED

Yes, sir.

JULES

Well, you're only young once. How much do you want?

ALFRED

Five thousand, sir.

JULES

Here you are, you rascal.

ALFRED

Thank you, sir.

JULES

And then?

ALFRED

I'd find out Jeannine was a tramp.

JULES

And then?

ALFRED

And then I'd go on a long journey to forget her. I'd try this place—that place—and then I'd wind up here. I'd walk into this shop. I'd see *her*. She'd see me. I'd wire you—my stepfather. "Have found *the* girl. We want your blessing."

JULES

Bless you, my children. Come home. All is forgiven.

ALFRED

Now do you see why it was all his fault?

JULES

Of course! The Judge should have given you the Legion of Honor and put the poker in the Louvre as a national monument.

(ALFRED *looks in mirror.*)

MARIE LOUISE

(*Enters, dressed for church, carrying hat, gloves, prayer book*)

Good morning. (*The men respond. She goes to table*) What are you writing?

JOSEPH

(*Covering his work*)

My memoirs.

(MARIE LOUISE *stares at* ALFRED.)

MARIE LOUISE

Oh, your jacket.

ALFRED

It's Paul's.

MARIE LOUISE

I know. Did he give it to you? You look very handsome.

ALFRED

I do?

MARIE LOUISE

Of course, Paul wears clothes with such—distinction. Such elegance.

ALFRED
(*Glumly*)

Yes.

MARIE LOUISE
But you look very nice. What is your name? You know, I don't even know any of your names.

ALFRED
Alfred.

MARIE LOUISE
You look very nice, Alfred. (*As she turns to* JULES, ALFRED *walks away*) And you are—?

JULES
Papa Jules.

JOSEPH
I'm Uncle Joseph.

MARIE LOUISE
I'm going to Mass. Will you still be here when I get back?

ALFRED
Yes.

MARIE LOUISE
(*To* ALFRED)

I want to thank you for—well—for everything you said yesterday. About Paul, I mean. You were right, you know. I was a fool to doubt him. Oh, I know he'll never love me as I love him. After all, I'm only a small part of his life. He has so many interests. But I don't mind. I want so little. Even his uncle must know that.

JOSEPH

His uncle knows everything now. I think you'll find he's acquired wisdom overnight. In fact, he's a changed man.

(*Beams.*)

MARIE LOUISE
(*Puzzled*)

He is? How?

JULES

You'll be late for Mass.

MARIE LOUISE

Since you're so anxious to get me off to church, I'm going to say a little prayer to St. Anthony for all of you—and for myself.

(*Exits into shop.*)

JOSEPH

Done! (*Rising*) My masterpiece. My magnum opus! The codicil to Uncle Henri's will will be discovered here.

(*Puts it on bureau in a prominent position, and the writing materials in their place.*)

JULES

We have a will, but have we a corpus delicti? Suppose— now just suppose Adolphe missed him—or ignored him.

MY 3 ANGELS

ALFRED

Adolphe wouldn't let his pals down.

JULES
(*Doubtfully*)

I don't know.

JOSEPH

Shall we have a little bet?

ALFRED

I'm a sportsman.

JOSEPH

I'll hold the stakes.

JULES

Ten centimes our dear uncle's alive and snoring.

ALFRED
(*Giving coin to* JOSEPH)

Take you.

JULES

Right.

 (JOSEPH *gets coin from* JULES.)

ALFRED
(*Picks up cage at chair and goes toward* HENRI's *room*)

I'll go see.

JULES
(*Stopping him*)

Just a minute. I don't trust you. If he's still alive, you might bash his head in just to win a bet. You go, Joseph.

JOSEPH
(*Sits facing table*)

Me? I'm squeamish. I don't like looking at dead people. It offends me esthetically.

JULES

Somebody's got to go.

JOSEPH

You go.

JULES

Oh, no. I'm the Judge. I never look at my victims. I like to sleep nights.

JOSEPH

Well, somebody . . .

(MME. PAROLE *enters from the shop, wearing the same hat she wore in Act One, but a different dress. She carries an opened bottle of cognac and her purse.*)

MME. PAROLE

Well, making yourselves at home, aren't you?

JOSEPH

Sorry I didn't hear the bell. I'm M. Ducotel's new assistant. May I assist you?

MME. PAROLE

I want to see M. Trochard.

ALFRED and JULES

What?

JOSEPH

M. Trochard?

MME. PAROLE

Oh, don't stare at me so stupidly. I know he arrived last night. I want to tell him a few things about M. Felix Duco-tel — the swindler! (*Showing the bottle*) Here, taste this cognac.

JOSEPH
(*Taking bottle*)

You want me to . . . Thank you. Season's greetings.

(*Gulps.*)

MME. PAROLE

Delicious, isn't it?

JOSEPH

Well, you've got to remember the thousands of miles this bottle has traveled—and the climate. Travel broadens us all, inclucing cognac.

MME. PAROLE

Really! How profound!

JOSEPH

I'll admit it has a little taste of—of . . .

MME. PAROLE
(*Exploding*)
There's no taste at all. It's plain water.

JOSEPH
Water? Madame exaggerates.

MME. PAROLE
So I'm exaggerating, am I? Read that label!

JOSEPH
For window display purposes only.

MME. PAROLE
Of all the outrageous . . . Ruining my Christmas!

JOSEPH
This is the wrong label. You don't think a company in its right senses would send a sample bottle thousands of miles. For what? This is a sound cognac, Madame. I say that not only as a merchant, but as a connoisseur.

MME. PAROLE
Are you mad? Read that label.

JOSEPH
Do you believe everything you read?

MME. PAROLE
Assassin.

JOSEPH

Please, Madame, no personalities.

MME. PAROLE

I want to see M. Trochard.

JOSEPH

Somebody should see M. Trochard. (*Putting bottle on table*) It might as well be you. (*Indicates to the left*) Please. This way, Madame. (*She starts toward the kitchen.* ALFRED *blocks her way at the same time as* JOSEPH *speaks*) No, no. Right in *here*.

(*Points to* HENRI's *room.*)

MME. PAROLE
(*Doubtfully*)

He's in there?

JOSEPH

Don't worry, Madame. It's not his bedroom. He's converted it into his office. M. Trochard is famous for converting everything into an office. Even his church pew on Sundays. (*She knocks*) Don't bother knocking. He may not hear you. Step right in, Madame.

MME. PAROLE

You're sure it's all right?

JOSEPH

Of course. After all, Madame, it's very important for you to see M. Trochard. The cognac is just an excuse. You've come because your husband is unhappy in the Customs Service and wants to be a merchant again. He wants to take over this shop. You want to help him get it.

MME. PAROLE

Of all the . . .

(*She enters* HENRI's *room.*)

JOSEPH

We'll soon know.

JULES

This is one bet I hope to lose.

(MME. PAROLE's *suppressed shriek is heard.* ALFRED, *with extended hand goes to* JOSEPH, *who pays off the bet.* MME. PAROLE *enters from the room, dazed.*)

MME. PAROLE

He's dead!

JOSEPH
(*Apparently astonished*)

What?

JULES

Did you say dead, Madame?

MME. PAROLE

I'm going to the police. If you scoundrels had anything to do with this, you'll pay for it.

JOSEPH

Madame, if you go to the police, we'll have to tell them—

144

MME. PAROLE

Tell them what?

JOSEPH

That we saw you coming out of his bedroom after your rendezvous.

MME. PAROLE

Rendezvous?

JULES

Madame, what were you doing in his bedroom?

MME. PAROLE
(*Indicating* JOSEPH)

He told me . . .

JOSEPH

It'll make a fascinating story. So romantic!

JULES

Shocking affair! Noted financier expires in ecstasy!

MME. PAROLE

But .

JOSEPH

A happy death. Madame, you have nothing to reproach yourself for. You gave yourself to him to help your husband. Your husband will understand. Your husband stayed up all last night on the ships working for you. And you stayed up all night here working for him.

MME. PAROLE

How dare you?

JOSEPH

Back of every successful man is a devoted wife! Yes, we have quite a story to tell the police. Shall we go along with you?

(*He backs toward shop entrance.*)

MME. PAROLE
(*Weakly*)
I'm not going to the police. I'm going home.

JOSEPH

By the way, I just remembered. You have a bill. Quite a large bill. It's time you paid.

MME. PAROLE

I'll take care of it.

(*She tries to leave. He stops her.*)

JOSEPH

How about a little something on account. (*Eyeing her bag*) I'll bet you have a few hundred francs there. Yesterday was payday for the Customs and you have a model husband. Turns his pay right over to you.

MME. PAROLE

I haven't any money with me.

(*As she backs away from him, she runs into* JULES.)

JOSEPH

I'll bet you have. Let's look together.

(*As she turns to look at* JULES, JOSEPH *seizes her bag.*)

MME. PAROLE

How dare you?

JOSEPH

What'd you say?

MME. PAROLE
(*Frightened*)

Nothing. (*As* JOSEPH *is going through the contents of the bag*) I need that money. I've some shopping to do...

JOSEPH

Don't tell me this is the only shop that gives you credit!

MME. PAROLE

Certainly not!

JOSEPH
(*Fishing out bills*)

I was right. Here we are. Three hundred francs. Congratulations, Madame. (*Hands her the bag*) I'll credit them to your account.

MME. PAROLE

But . . .

JOSEPH

Don't forget your cognac. (*Gives her bottle*) Keep it well corked and at room temperature. I recommend you use a snifter. Warm it with your hands to bring out the bouquet. And sip—don't swill!

(MME. PAROLE *exits, into shop, bewildered, frightened.* JULES *and* JOSEPH *chuckle.* JOSEPH *places the money in the cash box in the bureau drawer.*)

JULES
(*To* ALFRED)
You'd better get Adolphe.

ALFRED
Right.

JOSEPH
Use a towel on Adolphe.

ALFRED
I'll handle Adolphe.
(*Exits.*)

JULES
Godspeed.

JOSEPH
(*Going toward* JULES)
I say this objectively — Despite his sudden repentance, I think the world will be a better place without our dear uncle.

JULES
(*Hands him his mug*)
Still we face the old, old problem—Does the end justify the means?

JOSEPH
(*Puts mug on table*)

Of course.

JULES

I wonder.

JOSEPH

My philosophy is simple. If I perpetrate an outrage, it's justifiable. It's moral! It's noble! If someone else does it— it's an outrage.

(ALFRED *enters from* HENRI's *bedroom.*)

ALFRED

I can't find Adolphe!

JULES
(*Galvanized*)

What?

JOSEPH

Did you look in the bed?

ALFRED

Of course.

JULES

We've got to find him.

ALFRED

I looked everywhere. The window is shut tight. He may have crawled back in here.

(JULES *quickly rises and looks under chair cushion, then under the chair.*)

JOSEPH

We can't leave Adolphe loose. The poor little thing has no judgment when he bites. How can he differentiate between good and evil without us to guide him?

ALFRED
(Anxiously)

Maybe Adolphe's crawled off somewhere — sick — maybe he's dying . . .

JOSEPH

It's possible. Our dear Uncle was highly indigestible, even for a snake.

>   (*All three are looking as* PAUL *enters.* JOSEPH *and* ALFRED *are on their knees.* JULES *is searching to the left.*)

PAUL

Where are my . . .

JOSEPH
(Sees him, straightens up)

We were just looking for a collar button.

PAUL
(Stares at ALFRED*)*

What the devil are you doing with my jacket?

JOSEPH

The valet was just brushing it, sir.

PAUL

Does he have to wear it to brush it?

JOSEPH
It's a quaint local custom he's acquired. Alfred, take the gentleman's clothes to his room. And while you're there, I suggest you look for the collar button.

(*He undulates his hand at* ALFRED *as he exits.*)

PAUL
What collar button? Mine?

JOSEPH
No. A native product.

PAUL
I can't wait to get out of this damn country.

(*Exits, following* ALFRED.)

JOSEPH
(*Going to ladder and climbing it*)
It just occurred to me. We should look in the rafters. Adolphe likes trees—maybe he likes rafters. If he's strolled out into the garden, we're going to have a sweet job finding him.

(EMILIE *enters.*)

EMILIE
Looking for something?

JOSEPH
Yes, Madame—a collar button.

EMILIE
On the ceiling?

JOSEPH

Like other laws, the law of gravity doesn't always work. (*Climbing down the ladder*) If you will excuse me, I will continue my exploration in the Garden of Eden, looking hither and thither for the source of all our human wisdom.

(*Exits to garden.*)

EMILIE

(*Takes cup and saucer from bureau*)
What a strange man! Is M. Trochard still asleep?

JULES
(*Nodding*)

Dead—to the world.

(*She starts to sit in chair.* JULES *quickly stops her, picks up the chair, examines it, taps it on the floor, then, sure* ADOLPHE *is not on it, places the chair for* EMILIE *to sit. She does.* JULES *continues to look for* ADOLPHE.)

EMILIE
(*Pouring her coffee*)
You'll be leaving us today, won't you?

JULES

Yes, Madame. We'll be off soon—all four of us, I hope.

EMILIE

Four?

JULES

Adolphe, our pet.

EMILIE
(*Shuddering*)
Oh! (*After pause, during which she pours coffee for him*)
It's been interesting—your visit here.

JULES
(*Turns to her*)
It's been interesting for us, too.
(*Picks up his mug.*)

EMILIE
I want you to know—I don't know how to say this—but
I want you to know that I don't blame you for what you
did. (JULES *listens, puzzled*) That isn't what I meant to say.
About your wife, I mean. It may console you a little to know
that others, too, have these impulses—wild, almost uncon-
trollable impulses. I had such an impulse last night, as I was
trying to fall off to sleep.

JULES
You? You wanted to kill somebody?

EMILIE
Henri—M. Trochard.

JULES
(*Moving closer*)
Him? You wanted to kill him?
(*He begins laughing.*)

153

EMILIE

Oh, I know you think me ridiculous.

JULES

Not a bit.

EMILIE

It's absurd, of course.

JULES

Of course. Just how did *you* plan to exterminate M. Trochard?

EMILIE

My crime was all in my mind.

JULES
(*Smiles*)

Of course. No, you could never do it, Madame — under any circumstances. Think it? Yes. Perhaps even plan it. But actually do it . . .

(*Shakes his head.*)

EMILIE

Felix wouldn't even let himself think it. Poor Felix.

JULES

Why poor Felix? He's happy. And you're not unhappy.

EMILIE

I suppose not. I know that in a few hours, many dreadful things may happen. We may be shipped back to France,

154

penniless, with no prospects, nothing. God knows what we'll do. But somehow, I find myself echoing Felix: "Things will work out somehow. There's always hope."

JULES
He *is* right. Hope is everything. Even we have hope. We hope to escape, although we know we'll never do it. We hope for a pardon, although we know we'll never get it.

EMILIE
You know, sometimes I can't help wondering if I wouldn't have made a better wife for a man who wasn't a child — someone who didn't believe in fairy tales — who depended not on others, but on himself—and a little on me.

JULES
Men like that have no reason to marry.

EMILIE
You did.

JULES
Me? I believed in fairy tales, too—and when I stumbled on reality, I killed. You know what *I* was thinking when *I* finally fell off to sleep last night?

EMILIE
What?

JULES
I was thinking—if I had married a woman like you—well, I wouldn't be here.

155

EMILIE
(Touched, excited)

More coffee?

JULES

Thank you.

(Extends his mug.)

EMILIE

I'm beginning to wonder what is the matter with me this morning. I'm really feeling—thinking—saying—the most absurd—ridiculous . . .

JULES

Thank you for saying them.

EMILIE

I'm beginning to believe I'm the romantic—not Felix.

JULES

Yes .

EMILIE

I'm really not myself.

JULES

Thank you for this Christmas—it'll be a treasured memory. A man in my position doesn't store up many memories —and you—when you get back home to your Brittany—to the kind of home you should have—all this will be an amusing story for a dull dinner party.

156

EMILIE

I don't see a future of dinner parties, dull, or otherwise.

JULES

Remember: Hope! Things will work out somehow. (PAUL *enters*) Perhaps *he'll* work them out.

(EMILIE *looks up, startled.* JULES *gets cup and saucer from bureau, pours coffee and takes cup to* PAUL.)

PAUL
(*Kisses her hand*)
Good morning, Madame.

EMILIE

Paul, it's nice to see you.

PAUL

I'm sorry I missed you last night.

EMILIE

That's quite all right.

PAUL

That's a strange valet you have.

EMILIE

Valet?

JULES

Alfred!

PAUL

He's standing on the bed in his muddy sandals and star-ing at the ceiling.

JULES

He's looking for native wild life. He's a great student of nature.

(FELIX *enters.*)

FELIX

Where—Where is Henri?

(JULES *hands* FELIX *cup and saucer. He puts it on table.* EMILIE *pours.*)

EMILIE

He's still asleep.

PAUL

Asleep? (*Puts cup on table*) But that's impossible.

EMILIE

Why?

PAUL

He never sleeps this late. (*Looks at his watch*) He's al-ways up at six-thirty. No matter where he is. No matter how late it is when we go to bed. I don't understand it. (*Goes to* HENRI's *door*) I'm sure he'd want me to wake him. He said he had a heavy schedule.

(*Knocks on door.*)

158

FELIX
Well . . . Why not let him sleep?

PAUL
Then he'll think *I* overslept. I'd better go in and see.

(PAUL *exits into* HENRI's *room.*)

EMILIE
I hope nothing's happened.

JULES
Do you?

FELIX
Beautiful day. (*Looks at thermometer*) Only 104.

(ALFRED *enters, shakes his head.* JULES *signals him to wait quietly. There is a pause before* PAUL *enters, dazed.*)

FELIX
What's the matter?

PAUL
(*Moving away from door*)
My uncle—is—is—dead.

(EMILIE *rises.*)

ALFRED
Dead as a mackerel. But where the hell is . . .

(JULES *quiets him quickly, as he goes to table, busies himself with arranging the dishes on the tray.* AL-FRED *exits to garden.*)

EMILIE
(Rises)

Paul . . .

FELIX

Dead . . .

PAUL

His heart . . . It must have been his heart!

JULES

Did he have one?

EMILIE

Felix!

PAUL

I don't understand it. His doctors said he would live to be ninety!

JULES

He can sue his doctors for breach of contract.

FELIX

I'd better . . .

 (Goes into HENRI's *room.)*

EMILIE

I can't believe it!

PAUL

I don't understand it.

 (Follows FELIX *into room.)*

EMILIE

I must be dreaming.

JULES

You see, Madame, it isn't necessary to kill. Fate always arranges for the triumph of good over evil.

EMILIE
(*Stunned*)

He's dead!

JULES

Uhuh! No need for violence—no guilt—no self-reproach!

EMILIE

I can't help feeling a little—guilt. For even thinking . . .

JULES

In civilized countries, thinking is not a crime.

(FELIX *enters, followed by* PAUL.)

EMILIE

I'm so confused I no longer know where I am.

FELIX

It's so . . . It's terrible.

EMILIE

I think I'll go to my room.

JULES

A very good idea.

FELIX

Of course, darling. (*She exits*) I'll get a doctor to take care of the formalities. Paul, will you stay here, my boy? (JOSEPH *enters from garden with* ALFRED. JULES *goes to them*) I'll be back as soon as I can . . .

JOSEPH

I've just heard the news. We've lost a great man.

FELIX

I would never have forgiven myself if I'd deceived him last night.

JOSEPH

You were right. Once more we see that virtue is its own reward.

FELIX

Extraordinary. To die so suddenly.

(FELIX *exits into shop.*)

JOSEPH

The Lord giveth, the Lord taketh away.

(*He and* ALFRED *look about, still seeking* ADOLPHE. PAUL *starts toward* HENRI's *room. As he reaches the door he becomes aware that the three convicts have their eyes on him.*)

PAUL
(*Mopping his brow elegantly*)

What a thing to happen. I can't believe it. This is dreadful!

JULES

May I offer my sympathy?

PAUL

Thank you.

JOSEPH

Your uncle's death must be a great loss to you. I speak emotionally—not financially.

PAUL

Oh, yes . . .

JOSEPH

A great loss. (*Makes his way to bureau where he has left the forged note*) Oh, there seems to be a note here for you.

PAUL

For me?

JOSEPH

Here it is.

(*Taking it to him.*)

PAUL

Thank you. (*Takes it. Stares at writing*) From Uncle Henri?

JOSEPH

I wouldn't know. (PAUL *opens envelope.* JOSEPH *watches him warily, then casually*) I hope you didn't mind our little joke last night?

PAUL
(*Absently, staring at note*)

Little joke?

JOSEPH

The episode in the garden—under the bougainvillea—the bench . . .

PAUL

Oh, not at all. (*Stares at letter*) It was very pleasant—very . . .

(*His voice trails off as he studies letter, then crumples it and is about to tear it up.*)

JOSEPH
(*Seizing his hand*)

That's no way to treat a letter from your Uncle Henri—and he barely cold in his bed.

(JULES *and* ALFRED *move to table.*)

PAUL

Let me go . . .

JOSEPH

All communications from the deceased must be preserved. Have you no respect for the law? (*Straightening out the letter*) All communications! No matter how trivial . . . (*Pretends to study it*) And this doesn't seem trivial at all. Not at all! (*Gasps*) A dying man's last request—his last gasp. A voice from the grave!

JULES

Really?

PAUL

I'm—so upset naturally that—I didn't understand it . . .
I . . .

(He gets up to reach for the letter, but JOSEPH
passes it to JULES.)

JOSEPH

It's clear. (*To* JULES) It's clear to you, isn't it?

JULES
(Pretending to read)

I have a curious premonition . . . to restore to Felix Ducotel, my cousin . . . Be happy as I was not. Be honest, as
I was not . . .

(Hands letter to JOSEPH.)

JOSEPH
(Glaring at PAUL)

Your fiancée's father! Cheating *him!* Cheating the dead!
Sir, you're a cad!

ALFRED

With all that money he's inheriting! He wants more—
the swine!

PAUL

I have every intention of respecting my uncle's wishes.

JOSEPH

Now that we have this codicil to his will securely in our
possession!

PAUL

I won't contest it, I assure you. I repeat: I respect my uncle's wishes. If the document is genuine!

JOSEPH

If? You doubt this document?

ALFRED

What about Marie Louise?

PAUL

What about her?

ALFRED

Are you marrying her?

PAUL

I don't see how that concerns you.

JOSEPH

(*Stopping* ALFRED *from attacking* PAUL)

We went to some considerable trouble last night to smooth the path of love.

PAUL

(*After pause*)

In this, as in all other matters, I shall be guided by my uncle's wishes.

JOSEPH

You realize, of course, that you're now free to do as you please.

PAUL

Yes.

JULES

You're rich—your own master . . .

PAUL

Yes.

JOSEPH

But Suzanne Audibert, whose complexion cleared up miraculously, still attracts you?

PAUL
(*After pause*)

Yes!

JOSEPH

Gentlemen, a strange thing has happened. His uncle didn't die after all. He lives on—in *him!*

PAUL

I find this conversation distasteful—and impertinent. Once and for all . . . My relations with Marie Louise are my business, not yours. I'm *not* free to do as I please . . . Wealth is a responsibility.

JULES
(*Going toward him*)

Get out! Before I forget myself!

PAUL

What?

ALFRED

I'd like to bash his head in.

PAUL

You can't intimidate me. I'll report you.

JULES
(*Ominously*)
Your uncle wanted to report us.

ALFRED

Yeah.

JULES

We don't like being reported.

ALFRED

No.

PAUL

I believe the authorities have ways and means of punishing scoundrels like you. I was planning to call on the Governor with my uncle. Now I'll go alone, and I'll tell him how his convicts behave. As for that—forgery . . .

JOSEPH

Forgery?

PAUL

Suddenly a note appears a moment after my uncle's death. Suddenly! Suddenly he's repentant. I'll tell you what *I* think. I think you concocted this little scheme. And if M. Ducotel was a party to this, and I suspect he was, you may tell him I shall demand an official inquiry. Handwriting experts. And you can also tell him I'm going to have his books audited. A man capable of forgery is also capable of embezzlement! Now, with your permission, I'm going to pay my respects to the dead.

(Exits into HENRI's *room. There is a long silence, during which* JULES *moves to right of table,* JOSEPH *moves to above table,* ALFRED *goes to door of* HENRI's *room, glaring.)*

JULES

Shall we hold another trial?

JOSEPH

Now, please, not *two* accidents!

ALFRED

Why not?

JOSEPH

We'll never get away with it. Besides we've lost our executioner.

ALFRED

I'll do this job myself.

JULES

No, Alfred. Don't lose your head.

JOSEPH

No! Very distasteful business—the guillotine.

169

ALFRED

He doesn't deserve to live.

JOSEPH

That isn't the issue. The issue is: Do *we* deserve to live? The answer, in my slightly prejudiced opinion, is: yes.

JULES

At least we want to—even in solitary.

ALFRED

I'll do it all by myself. You won't be involved.

JOSEPH

They won't believe you.

JULES

And even if they did—we don't want to lose you. We belong together—we three.

ALFRED

All our work down the drain!

JULES

We tried.

JOSEPH

We failed. We've learned that virtue is not its own reward.

JULES

And that good does not always triumph over evil!

JOSEPH

For us, Christmas is over. We pack away the tinsel—store the tree—sweep away the debris—and complain vaguely of indigestion.

(PAUL *enters quickly, holding his hand.*)

PAUL

Call a doctor. Quick!

JULES

What's the matter?

PAUL

For Heaven's sake!

JOSEPH

What's wrong?

PAUL

I've just been bitten by a snake!

JOSEPH

What'd you say?

JULES

He said he'd just been bitten by a snake.

ALFRED
(*Beaming*)

How? Where?

PAUL

What does it matter? It hurts! A doctor!

JOSEPH
(*Going to him*)

Was it a little snake?

171

PAUL

Yes .

JOSEPH
(*Quickly*)

On the floor?

PAUL

No.

JOSEPH
(*More quickly*)

On the bed?

PAUL

No!

JOSEPH

On the dresser?

PAUL

No!

JOSEPH

On the ceiling?

PAUL

No! In his trousers—in the pocket!

JOSEPH

What were you doing with your hand in your uncle's pocket?

JULES

He was taking inventory!

(ALFRED *and* JULES *laugh. During the following,* PAUL's *pain and discomfort increase.*)

172

JOSEPH

This is no laughing matter. The young man's shown admirable industry—and thrift. His uncle may have had cash stowed away in his pockets—possibly only a few sous—rich men generally pride themselves on never carrying cash so that others will always pay their dinner checks, their cab fares, their tips—but the young man overlooks nothing!

PAUL

I want a doctor!

JOSEPH

Why waste your money?

PAUL

I don't feel well.

(JOSEPH, JULES *and* ALFRED *in a whispered conference.*)

JOSEPH

Damn nuisance to have him die in here.

JULES

Of course. Marie Louise'll be back soon. Imagine the shock. We've got to prepare her—and the family . . .

PAUL

What are you talking about? (*Starts toward shop entrance. Grabs on to ladder for support*) I want a doctor, I tell you.

JOSEPH

I have it. The garden! Let him die in the garden.

(ALFRED *goes to door of* HENRI's *room.*)

173

JULES

Good. We'll take him to the bench.

JOSEPH

Yes, the bench—the same bench as last night . . .

(JOSEPH *and* JULES *walk* PAUL *to the gate.*)

PAUL

You're always sending me to that damn bench!

(*The three exit into garden.* ALFRED, *with the coconut cage, goes into* HENRI's *room.* MARIE LOUISE *enters from the shop. She looks about.* ALFRED *reappears. He hides the cage behind him.*)

MARIE LOUISE

Oh, you're still here.

ALFRED

Yes .

MARIE LOUISE

Where's Paul?

ALFRED

Oh, here and there . . .

MARIE LOUISE

Is he—very upset?

ALFRED

Well, yes. I should say that Paul is very upset.

MARIE LOUISE

I met Father coming out of church. He told me.

ALFRED

Told you?

MARIE LOUISE

Don't you know—about Uncle Henri?

ALFRED

Oh, that one! Yes.

MARIE LOUISE

How awful!

ALFRED

I don't see why you should go into mourning — considering.

MARIE LOUISE

You don't understand. I said: How awful — because I should feel sorry, and I don't. Why are you staring at me?

ALFRED

Staring? No. I was just thinking of what you just said. (JOSEPH *and* JULES *enter from garden*) You know, you might think you're losing something, when you're really not. Sometimes you can be in love with something that doesn't even exist.

MARIE LOUISE

What are you hiding from me?

ALFRED

Well . . .

(*Looks to* JOSEPH *and* JULES *for help.*)

MARIE LOUISE

What's happened? Where's Paul? Are you trying to hint he—he doesn't love me? Is that it? Now that he's free, he doesn't want me. Is that it?

JOSEPH

He wants you—and loves you madly.

JULES

As much as you love him.

JOSEPH

He said something to us this morning that you should know.

MARIE LOUISE

What?

JOSEPH

He said: "Gentlemen," he said, "death has made me free to marry my adorable Marie Louise, and only death can part us now."

MARIE LOUISE

He said that?

JULES

Even more eloquently.

JOSEPH

If that's conceivable. He said—and these were his very words: "She doesn't realize how shy I am. How can I tell her nothing in this world matters as much to me as her love? Ambition? Wealth? Pouf!"

JULES
(*Snaps fingers*)
"For her," he said, "I'd dig ditches . . ."

JOSEPH
"Or pick pockets . . ."

JULES
Yes.

MARIE LOUISE
This is amazing. He's so reserved — generally — and he confided in *you*.

JOSEPH
The shock of his uncle's death—you know. He had to talk to someone.

MARIE LOUISE
And I wasn't here. Where is he?

JULES
I think he's with your mother.

MARIE LOUISE
Excuse me . . .
(*She exits.*)

ALFRED
(*Puts the cage on bureau*)
What's the idea?

JULES
It's a civilized custom to praise the dead. It helps the living.

177

JOSEPH

We wanted to give her a memorial. She'll need one.

JULES

Time will heal the wound. Let her at least cherish a memory.

JOSEPH

She's young. Someone'll come along. Someone always does.

JULES

It won't be you, Alfred, unfortunately. It could have been. It'll be someone else.

JOSEPH

The bell will ring—and there he'll be.

JULES

She won't love him as much as the mythical Paul—but she'll love him enough.

> (*Shop doorbell rings. The three start.* JOSEPH *rises, moves to* ALFRED. *But it is* FELIX *who enters, hangs up hat.*)

FELIX

What a time I've had. The doctor'll be along soon.

JOSEPH

Good. He has his work cut out for him.

FELIX

My wife still in her room?

JULES

Yes.

FELIX

I thought last night I'd be spending an entirely different kind of Christmas. Life is strange.

JULES

Isn't it?

FELIX

(*Cheerfully*)

Things work out somehow . . . (*Stops*) What am I saying? (*Guiltily*) I've got to see my wife.

(*Exits.*)

ALFRED

Well, back to the roof!

JULES

I guess so.

JOSEPH

It's too much to ask destiny to send along the young man we're waiting for at this precise moment. Still it would have been neater somehow. (*The shop bell rings. They look at each other, then step up toward the shop entrance, stop and wait. An extremely handsome young man in white naval uniform enters. They stare at him*) Yes?

LIEUTENANT

I beg your pardon, but there was no one in the shop. This is M. Ducotel's, isn't it?

179

JULES

It is.

LIEUTENANT

I suppose you work for him.

JOSEPH

We do.

LIEUTENANT

I've just landed, and I have a letter of introduction from friends in Cherbourg. May I see him?

JOSEPH

Forgive a question, sir. Are you married?

LIEUTENANT

I beg your pardon?

ALFRED

Well, are you?

LIEUTENANT

No. Why?

JULES

We were just wondering.

JOSEPH

You'll have to make certain allowances—have a little patience—You've chosen a rather peculiar time to appear.

LIEUTENANT

Peculiar?

JOSEPH

There's been a death here . . .

JULES

Two, in fact . . .

LIEUTENANT

I'm sorry to hear that.

JOSEPH

You needn't be.

LIEUTENANT

Perhaps I could come back later.

JOSEPH

Oh, no, no. Don't move.

JULES

Life's too short. Have a chair.

LIEUTENANT

But . .

JOSEPH

Sit down, sir.

(*The* LIEUTENANT *moves toward the chair.* MARIE LOUISE *enters and as she moves toward the garden comes face to face with the young man.*)

MARIE LOUISE
(*Seeing stranger*)

Pardon me . . . (*Crosses to gate below table. The* LIEUTENANT *turns to watch her*) Why didn't you tell me Paul was in the garden? There he is. He's sitting out there on the bench. He looks as if he's fallen asleep, (*Turns to the three convicts*) waiting for me . . .

JOSEPH

It's nice to know someone's waiting for you.

(*Looks at* LIEUTENANT.)

MARIE LOUISE
(*Smiles*)

Yes.

(*She exits to garden.*)

LIEUTENANT

Was that Mademoiselle Ducotel?

JOSEPH

Uhuh.

LIEUTENANT

She's charming!

ALFRED
(*Turns to him*)

Yes, she is.

JOSEPH

You're charming, too.

LIEUTENANT

I beg your pardon?

JOSEPH

You even look intelligent, which is more than we'd hoped for.

(*The harmonica is heard playing in the garden.*)

LIEUTENANT

Well, now, really!

JULES

Sit down. Relax. Close your eyes. You've got nothing to do—except wait.

(ALFRED *picks up his hat at foot of ladder then goes to bureau.*)

LIEUTENANT

If I closed my eyes, I'd be asleep in a minute. I was up all night on the ship.

JOSEPH

Well, then, sleep, sir. Sleep. (*Harmonica more distinct*) There's your lullaby.

(LIEUTENANT *closes his eyes.* JULES *gets his hat from box,* JOSEPH *gets his from table under the mirror, and both move to ladder. When there, the three turn back for one last look at the sleeping* LIEUTENANT. FELIX *enters, followed by* EMILIE.)

FELIX
(*Staring*)

Who's he?

183

JOSEPH

The future.

(MARIE LOUISE's *cry is heard.*)

EMILIE

Marie Louise!

(*Moves toward garden, exits, followed by* FELIX.)

JOSEPH

She's found happiness—and doesn't know it. She's only twenty, and she doesn't realize happiness wears many disguises.

(*Looks at* LIEUTENANT, *who hasn't stirred.*)

ALFRED
(*Picks up cage from bureau*)
Come, Adolphe.

JOSEPH
(*Starting up the ladder*)
Well, Your Honor, didn't we have a wonderful Christmas?

JULES

Yes, we did.

JOSEPH

Let's do it again next year.

The three angels climb up the ladder as

THE CURTAIN FALLS

184

WS - #0075 - 140621 - C0 - 229/152/11 - PB - 9780265086056 - Gloss Lamination